THEY LOOKED FOR A CITY

Yente at seventeen

THEY LOOKED FOR A CITY

LYDIA BUKSBAZEN

The Friends of Israel Gospel Ministry, Inc.
P. O. Box 908, Bellmawr, New Jersey 08099

THEY LOOKED FOR A CITY

Lydia Buksbazen

Copyright © 1955 by The Friends of Israel Gospel Ministry, Inc. Bellmawr, NJ 08099

Thirteenth Printing 2008

Library of Congress Catalog Card Number: 58-17705
ISBN-10 0-915540-15-0
ISBN-13 978-0-915540-15-0

Illustration concept: Thomas E. Williams
Illustration: Kathy Teal Morris
Layout design: Lori Winkelman

Visit our Web site at *www.foi.org*.

Dedicated to the Memory of

MY MOTHER

"I thank my God upon every remembrance of you."

Foreword

THE WRITING OF THIS BOOK is the fulfillment of a long-cherished hope to put down on paper the story of my family from the latter part of the 19th century to the Second World War.

They Looked for a City is the saga of a Hebrew-Christian family tossed by all kinds of national and personal storms, yet always emerging on the crest of each menacing wave, as if carried by the hand of a merciful God and the force of their faith. It is a pilgrim story of real people whose lives were marked by a two-fold stigma and a two-fold privilege—that of being Jews as well as believers in the Messiah of Israel, Jesus.

At the center of this family chronicle is my beloved mother Yente, because to me she personifies something that is so precious and peculiar—the heart of a Jewish mother and the impact of her faith upon her family and all those who came in contact with her. She was truly a daughter of Abraham, not merely by physical descent, but by faith also, for like the patriarch of her people, she too "looked for a city which hath foundations, whose builder and maker is God" (Heb. 11:10). Her life, suffused and permeated by the spirit of her Lord, was a blessing to many. It is my sincere hope that the colorful story of her eventful life will continue to bring encouragement and help to those who meet her through the pages of this book.

Now at last Yente has entered the blessed city of her longings, preceded there by her beloved son, my brother Jacob, and followed by her life companion, my father Benjamin. It is my prayer that those of us who are still on the pilgrim path may, in God's own time, join them in the city where there are no tears and that is lighted by the presence of Christ our Savior.

Come, my friend and reader, I will take you into a strange and partly lost world—into Czarist Russia, Poland, and Germany of a past generation, where millions of Jews lived, suffered, dreamed, hoped, and perished. Theirs was a fascinating world, steeped in the ancient ways and traditions of the Jew, shaped and fashioned by an ever-pressing hostile and sometimes destructive environment.

I will take you to Holland, and I will then introduce you to the people of England, grimly braving the terrors of two world-shattering wars. We will meet masses of people and individuals, some kindly, generous, gracious—God's kind of people. But we will also meet others—the hard, the heartless, the completely ruthless.

All of these people have one thing in common: They are not literary, fictional characters but real people. The tale of their lives is not spun with the ingenious threads of a fertile imagination; it is real. Here savagery and human brutality meet face to face with Christ-inspired saintliness and the faith that moves mountains and overcomes all obstacles. It is a story stranger than fiction, and I earnestly hope it will prove helpful.

On the background of this colorful canvas is etched the unusual and sometimes breathtaking experience of my own people.

They Looked for a City could never have been attempted were it not for the wise and loving help of my dear husband Victor Buksbazen, who, by his unfailing encouragement and with his talents as a writer, helped me continually, editing and correcting each chapter. Much of his own personal and unique knowledge and deep insight into Jewish life, thought, and background have gone into the making of this book.

Here is a testimony of faith, spelled out in human lives, the truth that King David, the sweet singer of Israel, once so beautifully described: "They who trust in the LORD shall be as Mount Zion, which cannot be removed, but abideth forever" (Ps. 125:1).

Lydia Buksbazen

Contents

THEY LOOKED
FOR A CITY

1

Jakob and Rachel

J AKOB GLASER WAS A RUSSIAN JEW who, in the middle of the 19th century, was kidnapped as a child and conscripted for compulsory military service in the army of the Czars. He served in the Russian army for the greater part of his life, about 25 years. His was an exciting, hard life—colorful but short. Wherever his military duties took him, his devoted wife Rachel, his three daughters, and his son went with him. The children were born in the living quarters of various Russian garrisons in the Caucasian Mountains. His entire mode of life reflected the typical Russian soldier. Even his appearance was Russian—tall, blonde, blue-eyed, big-boned, rather un-Jewish looking. Although he lived in a Gentile world, he always craved to return to a Jewish environment and finish his life as a Jew among fellow Jews. A strange fear gripped him that he might become lost to his people and die among strangers. His wife, a devout Jewess, loving mother, and wife, bore the hard, unsettled life without complaint—always seeking to bring comfort to her family wherever the army transferred them but missing the religious life that a pious Jewish woman craves for her family.

Thus it was that Jakob brought his family to the small city of Siedlce, a garrison city about 50 miles from the capital of Warsaw in Russian Poland. There they settled in a modest home, seeking to take root, weary of traveling, but happy in

1

the thought that at last their journey was ended and they could pursue their daily life in an environment that would include worship in the synagogue, instruction for the children, and a day of rest on the Sabbath.

However, they realized little of their dreams when Jakob, weakened by his many years in the service, became the victim of an epidemic that struck down hundreds. And so Rachel Glaser assumed the task of mothering and fathering her four young children.

Her dominant ambition was to teach her son Mottel (short for Mordecai) a trade. More than anything, she feared that he might follow in his father's footsteps and join the Russian army, there to lead the same kind of life that had shortened Jakob's life. Bravely she struggled to give the children the minimum of education, for in those days education was a luxury only the rich enjoyed.

Rough-Riding Cossacks

At that time there was great unrest in Russian Poland. For over a century Poland had been ravaged by her powerful neighbors and divided among the three great empires of the day—Russia, Germany, and Austria. The Poles, always patriotic to the point of self-destruction, again and again rose up against the Russians and their other oppressors. These outbreaks were mercilessly suppressed, with many Poles being killed and thousands deported and sent to the dreaded Siberia. To strike terror into the hearts of the Polish rebels and the restless population, the Russian police and the Cossacks were given a free hand. Of course, the Jews, as usual, became the scapegoats. The Russians, to divert attention from themselves, incited the Poles against the Jews according to the ancient recipe—divide and rule. The unhappy and frustrated Poles vented their malice on the helpless Jews, and Russian-inspired pogroms often occurred.

Those were the days when the Cossacks, on their swift, fiery horses brought from the Steppes of Siberia, swooped down, like a bolt from the blue, upon unsuspecting and defenseless people, swinging their *nahaikas* (knotted leather thongs) or using their sabers indiscriminately in the streets of the Polish villages and cities.

A Jew dressed in his traditional long black coat, adorned with side curls, and covered with the velvet cap of the pious was a special attraction. Like a hunter at the sight of his prey, the Cossacks descended on the Jews, their horses' hoofs trampling down those who happened to be in their paths.

Death Under the Horses' Hoofs

During an attack by a Cossack detachment on the Jewish population in Siedlce, Rachel and two of her daughters were caught in the street. Seeing the Cossack rider approaching them, Rachel acted quickly. Throwing herself between her daughters and the Cossack, she bore the brunt of the thong lashes and was kicked on the head by the excited horse. The two girls took their bleeding and bruised mother home, but after several weeks she finally succumbed to a brain injury and ensuing paralysis. Such was the end of this brave and genteel Jewish woman, whose aim in life was to serve God as best she could and provide a home and daily bread for her family.

Sarah was the oldest daughter. She had always been her mother's right hand, taking her place at home when Rachel was earning a living and at her job when Rachel was sick. Quiet, unobtrusive, passionately fond of her two younger sisters and brother, she was the plodder, the realist. Mottel, the secondborn, had by now finished his apprenticeship in the shoe factory and was ready to go out into the world and earn his own living. Later he married and took his wife and children to South America, an adventure on which many young married men yearned to embark but which few had the courage or means to achieve.

Yente With the Golden Hair

The middle girl was Yente—golden-haired, fair-skinned, blue-eyed, Yente. She was the pride of the family. Her striking beauty was famous in the little town of Siedlce. And with her beauty went a strong character and an impelling personality.

She was indeed the sunshine of that little home. In spite of the daily struggle for existence, she always saw the sunny side of life and imparted to others that rare gift of accepting with a smile whatever came her way, be it joy or sorrow. Yente was an ambitious girl, and like her mother she early dreamed of a life without the daily fear of hunger and struggle. She was a hard worker and an outdoor girl.

When the weather was mild, she slept in the back yard or the neighbor's field. Early in the morning, even before dawn, she arose, washed herself in the icy cold brook running through the field, gathered wood for the fire, and brought water for the household. Life was indeed primitive in those days in Poland, yet looking at Yente, one could see no traces of roughness on her smooth white skin, no sign of fatigue on her fair young face.

Her love for children made her the village nursemaid. Whenever she had an opportunity (and there were many), she helped the village mothers by taking their babies and young children into the woods to pick berries and nuts. Then she returned the children to their mothers and was usually invited to share a meal, which she gladly accepted as payment for caring for the youngsters. At harvest time she offered her services to the farmers as a picker in the fields, again giving her an opportunity to be outdoors and breathe the fresh air, which to her spelled life. Her midday meal consisted chiefly of bread, milk, and fresh fruit.

The death of her mother, whom she loved above all others, was a blow that brought home to her for the first time the seriousness of life.

4

The youngest sister, Dora, not yet ten, was wholly dependent upon the support of her older sisters.

It became more and more apparent to Sarah as the days passed that their future was not in the small city of Siedlce. It was unthinkable that the three girls should remain in this garrison city alone, at the mercy of the thousands of soldiers who paraded the streets from early morning until late at night. The burden of responsibility for her sisters weighed heavily upon Sarah, and thus it was that she decided to take them to the capital city, Warsaw, to seek a living in the ghetto among their own Jewish people. In the big city they would be much safer than in Siedlce, and there would be greater opportunities for employment.

2

The Big City

I
T WAS SPRING 1896. The great day of their departure from Siedlce had been decided upon. It was inconceivable to their neighbors and friends that the Glaser girls were packing their few belongings and leaving the little town where they were known and loved by all.

First their friends tried to persuade them to change their minds, pointing out the dangers besetting young girls who ventured out on their own in a city as vast as Warsaw. Some even said they would share their last crust of bread with them, if only they would stay. But Sarah was not moved by their pleas.

Yente, a blossoming girl of 13 and rather mature for her years, was touched by the concern of their neighbors and, above all, by the entreaties of her young friends who loved her dearly. It was hard for her to part from these children who were so precious to her. Then there were the fields and orchards, every inch so familiar and precious; and the brook that ran through the neighbor's field seemed to say, *Stay on, stay on. I'll refresh you, I'll sing to you, and you will be happy here.* She had spent many hours on warm summer nights beside that brook. She had seen herself as in a mirror as she sat and dangled her feet in its cool water, refreshing as dew from Heaven—the brook was peculiarly her own.

She wondered how she could live in the great city where there were no fields, wild flowers, or brook. She thought of her mother whom she loved so dearly—the mother who had toiled for her children so patiently, the mother who had taught them to fear God and to love Him. Never again would she nestle in her mother's arms, feel her stroke her long plaits, and hear her say, "My child, it isn't what man makes that comforts, but what our great God has given to us that we should enjoy and treasure." Rachel was a simple but devout woman. She knew God with all her heart. "Children," she often said, "remember your Creator and worship Him. Never be too tired or too busy to give God His due." She instilled that simple creed into the minds and hearts of her children. Now Yente was to leave the place where her beloved mother was buried. Would she be unfaithful to her memory by doing so? Never again would she have the opportunity to visit the "eternal place," as the Jews called the cemetery, where her father and mother lay side by side. She wept at the thought.

For a girl of her age, she had great depth of feeling, and a wave of loneliness came over her. But Sarah insisted and finally prevailed upon her.

On a Polish Train

At last the day came when, sad good-byes having been said, the three girls boarded the slow, smoke-belching train that would carry them to Warsaw. What a tedious journey that was; it seemed endless. The carriages were filled with peasant families coming from and going to neighboring towns to dispose of their produce in the markets. Several women carried huge cans of milk on their backs fastened around their shoulders with coarse sheets. Some carried baskets containing eggs and dairy products or cackling hens. They shared their meals, eating the heavy black bread and smoked, garlicky pork sausages at which the Jewish passengers looked askance and turned away their heads—such abomination!

The Jews were going to the big city to visit relatives, buy goods for their small stores, find work, see the great rabbis, or study in the famous Talmudic colleges with which the city abounded.

Here and there some who did not have the necessary fare hid under the wooden seats in the car, and the women, with their wide skirts, obligingly covered them. The conductors were usually wise to such tricks and found them; however, ten *kopeekes* (a dime) took care of the matter, for the time being at least, until there was a change in the train crew.

Sarah and her sisters looked through the windows as fields of rich black soil seemed to run backwards—fields full of promise for a great harvest. The rye was green and luscious, and so was the wheat. Potatoes were peeping through the ground, and in between were red clover fields, rich fodder for the horses and cattle.

Here and there the girls saw peasant cottages with thatched roofs and farmers with their barefoot children standing in awe before the passing train.

In the Ghetto of Warsaw

Finally, after many hours, the great Warsaw railway station loomed before them, and they stood in amazement. The thrill of the big city held the girls spellbound. The profusion of gas lights in the streets (unknown in the murky and muddy environs of Siedlce), the noise of the horse-drawn *doroshkies* (cabs) as they rumbled along the cobbled streets on their ironclad wheels, the jingle-jangle of the horse-drawn trolleys, the bulky trucks drawn by big horses, the hustle and bustle of endless crowds hurrying to their duties or just sauntering about aimlessly, the big shops with show windows containing a variety of never-before-seen clothing and other fancy goods beyond the wildest dreams of these country girls—everything awed and numbed their senses. They felt lost in this strange and overpowering new world.

Fortunately a friend of Sarah's took them to a small room in the Jewish district, which she had managed to rent for them after much searching. Now they were in the heart of the Jewish ghetto, indeed in the very heart of European Jewry. Around them the streets swarmed with Jews, and all of them seemed to be such fine Jews.

Most of the men wore long black caftans and peculiar little black caps made of cloth or shiny black velvet, the headgear of the most pious. Their faces were adorned with side curls and flowing beards. Their eyes were sad and dreamy. It seemed as if 19 centuries of suffering and exile looked out through those tragic eyes. Here and there one could see a Jew in a great hurry, carrying his *talles* (prayer shawl) and the *phylacteries* used during the morning worship service. He was hurrying to make *minyan* (a quorum of ten Jews without which there could not be a public service) in the *Shul* (the Synagogue). Otherwise he would have to pray by himself, a procedure far less meritorious than partaking in the prayer of a *minyan*. Here and there were Jewish boys with delicately chiseled features accentuated by undernourishment and poverty, their long black coats revealing, as they skipped along in boyish fashion, the *talles kotten* (the four-fringed garment with long tassels) that was the mark of orthodoxy.

It did not take the girls long to realize that they would feel safer here than in the garrison town of Siedlce, where the drunken Russian soldiers and their abusive manners were nightmarish. *Surely*, thought Yente, *mother would approve of this move*, and the thought comforted her. She would work and earn money here.

Sarah already had a job in a furrier's workroom making fur caps, and Yente too would learn the trade. It was Sarah's intention to earn a living for her two younger sisters until they were old enough to provide for themselves, but Yente insisted on working immediately; therefore, Sarah apprenticed her, strangely enough, to a Gentile furrier. He had several children, and Yente was to look after the children part-time and learn the trade part-time.

This worked out well until payday when Yente's boss, an unreliable man who did not keep Sabbath for his Jewish employees or Sunday for himself and who drank away his profits, calmly told his employees they would have to wait for their pay until his next batch of work was completed. This did not please Sarah at all, and she kept Yente home to keep house until a more profitable opening came along. Sarah worked hard, often 16 hours or more a day, and took care of her sisters, watching over them like a mother.

Every week she brought home some new material, for they had very little in the way of clothing. She sat up for hours, and, with the help of Yente, sewed for them all, until the time came when they could step out among other girls not feeling too shabby. She even hired a high school girl to come in twice a week and tutor her sisters, hoping that this would give them a greater opportunity to earn a living when the time came. By the time Yente was 15, she was working beside Sarah, learning the trade, and bringing her earnings into the one room that was their home. Pooling their meager earnings, they somehow eked out a living.

In the rush of city life, memories of the past quickly grew dim. The new life crowded out the old. Yente was happy that at last she was able to work and share the financial burden with her sister. After saving for many months, Sarah had Yente measured for her first really elegant dress, made by a dressmaker, and her joy was complete.

A Sabbath Day

The girls always kept the Sabbath as their mother had taught them. On Friday afternoons, the work for the week completed, they scrubbed, washed, and tidied their home to give it a real Sabbath appearance. The table was covered with a white tablecloth, and Sarah, now the head of the family, kindled the Sabbath lights soon after sunset, just as her mother had done before her. She then covered her face with the palms of her hands and silently prayed a prayer of dedication to the God of Abraham, Isaac, and Jacob. As she did so, she recalled Rachel doing the same thing for so many years, both when her father was alive and later in her widowhood, and tears trickled through her fingers as she remembered her dear mother.

The girls then read short prayers from the prayer book, the portion appointed for women on the Sabbath. They had no obligation to go to the Synagogue, for this was a duty and privilege reserved for men who daily thanked God for the privilege, saying, "Blessed art Thou Lord our God who did not create me as a woman."

The smell of the Sabbath foods filled the little home. There was gefilte fish made of the chopped meat of fresh river fish such as carp, perch, or pike, flavored with a goodly portion of onions, salt, pepper, sugar, and egg yolk, added to hold it together. They kept the skin of the fish, filled it with the prepared fish meat, and simmered it in water with vegetables. The fragrance, so precious to Jewish nostrils, and to some of the Gentile neighbors as well, filled their home and the entire neighborhood on Friday afternoons.

Then there was the chicken prepared in the kosher way—soaked in water for a full hour and then salted for a half hour, so that no blood remained in the fowl, for God had commanded His people not to partake of the blood of slaughtered animals.

On the Sabbath table there was also *hallah*, an oval-shaped bread made with egg and sugar with a shiny brown crust.

Their prayers ended, the girls washed their hands according to the law of their ancestors by pouring water from a quart jug three times on clenched fists, first on the left hand and then on the right. Then they wiped their hands, said the appointed prayer, sat down at the table, gave thanks over the bread, and drank the *kiddush* wine (the wine of consecration). Finally, they proceeded with their meal. They were happy and proud of their achievements and independence, but deep and gnawing loneliness and sadness remained in their hearts. They were three orphan girls trying to put on a brave front in a strange world.

On high holy days, such as Yom Kippur (the Day of Atonement), the Passover, and the Feast of Tabernacles, they went to the Synagogue to attend the memorial services, a religious duty in which even women were expected to take part.

In the Synagogue they sat in the gallery looking down on the men beneath. The *chazen* (cantor), in a highly cultivated tenor voice, chanted the prayers, always facing east. The prayers with their ancient melodies and melancholic dirges made a profound impression on the sisters. The candles with their twinkling lights somehow reminded them of the souls of their beloved parents, and when the cantor chanted in somber tones, *El molai rahamim* (*Oh, God full of mercy*), the prayer for the departed souls, all the women and some of the men cried aloud, remembering their dead.

On Sabbath afternoons and evenings or on high holy days the girls went for a walk, as did all the young people, promenading along Nalewki Street, the main thoroughfare of the Jewish ghetto in Warsaw. Soon faces became familiar. Young people greeted one another with *Gut Shabes* (*Good Sabbath*) or *Gut Yomtov* (*a good holiday to you*). Friendships were made and romances blossomed. Small groups of friends went to nearby cafes for a glass of tea with lemon and tasty little cakes. If six hours had passed since their last meat meal, they had chocolate with whipped cream, a delight that only the more well-to-do could afford. The poorer indulged at the expense of the next morning's breakfast.

The Promenade

The three Glaser girls soon attracted attention not only because of the Sabbath promenade but also because a more beautiful girl than Yente could not be seen. Her fair complexion and long golden braids were the envy of all the teenagers, many of whom vied for a place to walk beside her so that they too might attract some of the attention so richly lavished on her.

It did not take long before young men asked Sarah for permission to walk out with Yente; but Sarah, a strict disciplinarian, rarely approved. During one of their walks, a handsome young man was pointed out to the girls, and they were told he was a neighbor who was very quiet and usually kept to himself. He was the son of a wealthy Jewish cabinetmaker whose shop and workrooms were within a stone's throw of the girls' home. Forty or more men worked in the shop.

Benjamin

Yente had often seen this young man and admired his quiet but poised manner. She also admired his good looks. He was a refined young man, somehow different from the others. When she saw him during the week, he was usually busy, in and out of his father's factory. He seemed to be self-possessed, and she imagined that he must be very accomplished. His features were regular; his dark hair and small mustache were always well-trimmed. She often wondered how he found time to be so well-groomed when he always seemed to be working.

This was Benjamin Sitenhof, the only son of one of the most respected Jewish families on Nalewki Street. She wondered if he had ever noticed her—probably not. After all, she was just one of the many girls he saw day in and day out. She shrank from meeting him, but it was too late. A friend introduced him to the Glaser sisters.

It was love at first sight, and a friendship quickly developed. Yente and Benjamin soon realized they would have much opposition from his family, for he was the promising and accomplished son of well-to-do people who would be able to marry a wealthy girl from a well-known and honored family. This was an accepted practice in Jewish life. Learning, wealth, and a good family were held in great respect. A "good family" meant descent from rabbinical luminaries and scholars. Matches were arranged by matchmakers who proposed to the parents of each party and enlarged upon the merits and virtues of the prospective bride and groom—for a monetary consideration, of course.

An accomplished young man would be entitled to a rich dowry, perhaps partnership in business with his father-in-law. If he were a scholar, he would be entitled to several years of *kest* (room and board in the in-laws' home until his course of study was completed and he was able to provide for his new family).

Benjamin was the apple of his father's eye. At 17 he was not only a master cabinetmaker and carpenter but the brains behind his father's business. He was also a studious young man, diligently studying the Torah, and old scholars often congratulated his father on Benjamin's accomplishments. Perhaps one day he might even become a rabbi and bring honor to his father's name. Pampered and idolized by his eldest sister, who mothered him after their mother's death, he somehow remained unspoiled and serious beyond his age.

Now he was confronted with a problem such as he had never faced before. All his needs and difficulties were taken care of by a loving father and doting sister, but this time he would have to decide for himself. One thing he knew: Come what may, he would marry Yente. Whatever the consequences, he felt he could shoulder them. Young and efficient, he felt capable of managing his own affairs. He was thrilled at the thought that, of all his friends, he was the one who had won the heart of the most beautiful girl in the Jewish area. Her sweet nature and natural beauty made a lasting impression on everyone who knew her.

Thirty years later when she returned to visit Warsaw, people still recognized her and cried, "Where are your lovely golden braids, Yente?"

Benjamin and Yente Elope

It was a shock to Benjamin's father, a venerable old man with a good reputation in his community, when his beloved son announced that he wished to marry Yente. At first he did not take him seriously, but he soon realized that the matter was serious indeed. Benjamin's sister Sima flew into a rage and vowed she would have Yente hounded out of town if he did not give up this mad idea. Undaunted, Benjamin secretly arranged the wedding in a little town not far from Warsaw.

The small town rabbi, dressed in full rabbinical regalia (shining black hat with broad brim, long black coat reaching to his ankles, and black silk sash), presided. Beside the rabbi and the prospective bride and groom, there were only a few witnesses present. The wedding canopy (*huppah*) was erected, and underneath it Benjamin said to Yente, as he slipped the wedding ring on her finger, "Thou art betrothed unto me according to the law of Moses and Israel." He then added the traditional words that God pronounced concerning His future ransomed bride, Israel:

> And I will betroth thee unto me forever; yea, I will betroth thee unto me in righteousness, and in justice, and in loving-kindness, and in mercies. I will even betroth thee unto me in faithfulness; and thou shalt know the LORD" (Hos. 2:19-20).

A glass was then broken, and the small company shouted *Mazol Tov! Mazol Tov!*—may you have good luck. Benjamin and Yente were now man and wife according to the Law of Moses and Israel.

The happiness of the young couple was great, but it was soon marred when Benjamin's family insisted that their marriage be annulled. Ominous clouds were gathering on their horizon. Yet in all these things, the hand of God led through sorrow and tribulation to a deeper and fuller knowledge of Himself that was to revolutionize their lives.

3

The Importance of *Yihes*

B ENJAMIN'S FATHER AND TWO SISTERS vehemently opposed his "misalliance," as they called the marriage. They could not imagine what had possessed him to marry Yente. What kind of dowry did she have? Who were her people? All she had was a pretty face and a pair of golden braids. True, she had a good face, clear blue eyes, and a well-formed chin that bespoke character and determination.

If she only had *Yihes*—a noble descent of which she could be justly proud. But she had no illustrious ancestors—no rabbis, no famous scholars, not even any outstanding and prosperous merchants. All she could boast of was her soldier father, a Jew who almost became a Russian. And she herself was just a country orphan who had to work hard with her hands to earn a bare living. Let her marry her own kind—not a fine, promising, brilliant young man "like our Benjamin"—his family said.

Of course, this attitude did not contribute to the happiness of the young couple. Love does not blossom readily in such soil. Sarah, Yente's sister, saw this very clearly and believed that the young people must get away from Warsaw if their marriage were to succeed and not be wrecked on the cliffs and rocks of family disapproval and hostility.

Get Thee Out

Further complicating the situation was the fact that things were not good for the Jews in the Russian Empire, of which Poland was a part in those days. The Cossacks were still riding high, and peasants and town people, cunningly incited by the Russian church and Czarist officialdom through malicious rumors and accusations, were participating in riots and bloody pogroms, swallowing up thousands of Jews. There was a wide wave of migration, a desire to get away from Russia and its oppression—anywhere, the farther the better. Many went to Germany, France, England, and faraway and fabulous America, the dream of thousands. There the streets, it was said, were paved with gold, and all trouble would end as soon as you set foot in that wonderland.

Sarah felt it was her duty to help her sister and brother-in-law. They were young—Yente 16 and Benjamin 17—and somebody had to take care of them. She left for England to prepare the way for Benjamin and Yente to follow as soon as she found work and a place for the young couple to live.

Sarah succeeded wonderfully in her task. She soon sent word for the young couple to follow, and in the spring of 1900 Benjamin and Yente left for England with high hopes for a bright future, not only for themselves, but for the child they were expecting.

Fortunately, in those days passports were not necessary. Only in later years did they become essential. "Man," they later said in Russia, "consisted of three parts—body, soul, and passport; and the most important of the three was the passport." But in the spring of 1900 the passport had not yet become an essential part of life.

Yente and Benjamin journeyed across the continent of Europe by train—third-class, which was no picnic in those days. The trains were dirty and overcrowded, and among the passengers were the young, the elderly, and even babies in their mother's arms. There was a real babel of languages and dialects, with Yiddish more than holding its own. Smoke and coal cinders drifted in through the doors and windows, adding to the discomfort and weariness of the passengers. All were hungry and red-eyed from lack of sleep. A stale odor of *machorka* (a cheap tobacco) and handmade cigarettes made the air thick and unbearable. The small compartments and corridors were crowded with people leaning against the windows eager to catch a glimpse of Europe (Russia was not considered part of Europe) or sitting on their bundles or cheap cardboard and fiber valises.

But this was not an unhappy crowd by any means. Most of them were young, full of excitement and expectancy. They were pioneers about to experience new adventures and conquer unknown worlds. *If we could only pierce the veil of the future and know what was going to happen at journey's end*—such were the thoughts pervading their minds.

If they were uncomfortable, tired, or hungry, it didn't matter because at the end of the journey golden opportunities awaited them—a new, exciting life. Once and for all they would be far away from hated Russia with its iniquitous laws, corruption, and maudlin sentimentality, which often changed rapidly into extreme cruelty. They would be free; they would be men among men.

Yente, as always, craved fresh air and open space more than food. She sat in the corridor for the greater part of the journey, peering out the window whenever she could gain the coveted position. The countryside looked beautiful and refreshing.

The White Gates of Heaven

The last lap of the journey, crossing the English Channel, was made by boat. This was a most exciting experience, as neither Yente nor Benjamin had ever seen the sea before. What a thrill it was to breathe in that first whiff of salty sea air, to see the endless expanse of water, to hear the mighty roar of the waves beating against the shore. Oh, the exultation! They wanted to shout for joy. Up the ramp they went, mingling with the medley of human beings and their endless bundles, as they eagerly sought to catch a glimpse of the distant shores of England. At last the white cliffs of Dover came into view, and it seemed to Yente that they were the white gates of Heaven, beyond which they would live in total happiness. Here her first child would be born in a free country. Here even a Jew was allowed to go about his business without fear of Cossack lashes and the engineered bloody pogroms of the incited mobs. Whether knowingly or not, they had always looked for such a city, and here it was just within their grasp. O happy thought!

And then came London, the metropolis of Europe. With awe they stepped out of the train into Victoria Station. They fairly caught their breath in amazement at the great luxurious trains and magnificent station restaurant they had glimpsed as they passed. It was a new world indeed.

And then there was Sarah. What a reunion! She was concerned about her little sister and bombarded her with questions. "Did you have a good journey? Are you feeling well?" The eyes of the newcomers spoke of their delight and joyful anticipation. Fortunately, a wise providence had not revealed to them the life of wandering, tribulation, joys, and sorrows they would be called upon to endure.

Petticoat Lane

Sarah took them to a small room on Leman Street off Whitechapel, which she had rented for them. She apologized for its size and explained that it would only be for a short time—until they could find larger quarters and Benjamin found a job. But Benjamin was a master craftsman in his trade, and he had no difficulty finding work as a carpenter.

They lived in the heart of the Jewish section of London. His work was so near home that he could even drop in for lunch.

As soon as they had rested from the journey, Sarah took them to Petticoat Lane, the great shopping street of the Jewish world. It was just like Nalewki Street in Warsaw, only more so. In shops and on the sidewalks they saw crowded stalls displaying everything one could imagine—all the things precious to the palate of good Jewish folk. There were large barrels of salted herring and pickles, smoked salmon, and black juicy olives, the aroma of which permeated the entire market. There was an abundance of fish from both the sea and the rivers.

Nearby a little Jewish man from Lithuania was selling *beigles*, round rolls with holes in the middle. At the top of his voice he exalted his wares, crying in Yiddish, "Fresh beigles, fresh beigles, straight from the oven. Refresh your souls." In Petticoat Lane the soul's delight and the body's pleasure mingled into one great Jewish harmony.

Nearby was a stand full of ties, socks, handkerchiefs, and other white goods and haberdashery, as well as a stall loaded with remnants of beautiful colored materials. Its owner was shouting as he displayed his multicolored wares, "Pick 'em up, pick 'em up. Dress like a queen for next to nothing."

There was a short crippled man hovering over a barrel of miscellaneous stockings, watching feverishly the dozen or so pairs of hands which dove down into his supply to match up a pair. If you found the matching stocking, the cost was only three pence. With an eagle's eye, he watched the hands lest one pair disappear without payment. When asked to help match a pair, he would shout back, "Tomorrow, tomorrow, come back tomorrow." This would bring forth a howl of laughter from the crowd as they knew his unchanging retort. Then there were the shops and stalls full of old and new clothing and yard materials—what wonderful bargains for the poorer people, both Jew and Gentile.

Yente stood as if hypnotized. The manner of these Jews was the same and yet so different from those she had left behind in Poland—the same features, the same faces, but strangely different. Bondage fell away, and an atmosphere of freedom pervaded the air. She felt at home among these people. Tears of joy came to her eyes as she thought, with a prayer of thankfulness in her heart, how privileged she was that her first child would be born in this blessed country. Her firstborn would be British.

In the distance Big Ben was booming out an evening hour, and nearby chimes answered with a joyful, harmonious chorus of high, clanging, ringing tones.

Sarah worked hard and insisted on paying the rent so that Benjamin's earnings could be saved for the anticipated doctor's fees and considerable expenses connected with the coming baby. Evenings were spent in their modest little room, and they enjoyed the twilight atmosphere while it lasted. When night came they often sat in the dark, either lacking or trying to save the pennies necessary for the gas meter. They talked about life back home in the old country, but already it seemed to be fading into the past, crowded out by and submerged into this new exciting life in the great throbbing metropolis of the world.

The Tempest

Yente was happy. But was Benjamin? A change soon came over him, and he often sat silently and pondered. How could Yente know what was going on in the mind of her young husband? How could she know that in his thoughts he was back in his father's spacious home, the pride of his family, his every wish acceded to almost before it was expressed. The truth was that life in London was not at all rosy. The little room in Leman Street was dingy and depressing. The cooking odors of the other tenants blended into one nauseating smell, from which he often withdrew and took a walk in wide Whitechapel Street, where he could at least breathe freely. A sixth sense warned Yente that her happiness was in peril.

Yente accompanied Benjamin on his walks as long as she could because she felt the lack of fresh air even more than he, but neither expressed their innermost thoughts for fear of making the other unhappy. Benjamin was hardly more than a boy suddenly brought face to face with the duties and burdens of manhood, burdens frightening and heavy for his slender shoulders.

In the evenings Sarah often came and sat with Yente while Benjamin was taking his walks. As time went on, it seemed that those walks grew longer and longer. Anxious for her sister's welfare, one evening Sarah decided to follow him. She saw Benjamin enter a house in the neighborhood, and in a short time she saw him come out in the company of two other people. To her amazement they were his older sister Regina and her husband. Now Sarah was able to put the pieces together. She knew that Regina was planning to go to America, and in all probability she had stopped in England on the way to the United States. But why hadn't Benjamin told them about her arrival? Why the secrecy? She felt hurt and was disappointed in him for the first time, and then fear gripped her heart. There must be a plot; something was going on. The family still wanted to separate Benjamin from her sister and either take him to America or send him back to Poland.

A premonition of fear held her rooted to the spot. How could she tell Yente? But, on the other hand, how could she keep it from her? Her baby was expected any day, and surely Benjamin would not listen to his sister at such a time. But Sarah had heard that Regina and her husband were heartless people and were known as troublemakers.

She went back to their little room; and when she arrived, out of breath, she was surprised to see a small group of people standing near the entrance. Quickly she made her way through the crowd, her heart pounding with fear. She realized the doctor and midwife were there. The baby had arrived, and she was not at her sister's side when she needed her most.

And where was Benjamin? No one knew. Sarah sent a neighbor to the address from which she had just returned, and soon Benjamin came.

"Mazol Tov, daddy! What a fine daughter you have, Benjamin. What are you going to call her? Elizabeth? Doesn't sound very Jewish, but it's all right. Come to think of it, isn't Elizabeth the slightly disfigured English for the good Hebrew name

Elisheva, meaning *the Lord has promised on oath*? Of course it is. Now He has kept His promise. Blessed be His name!"

Sarah was so glad that she did not have an opportunity to tell Yente of her distressing discovery. She would keep it to herself and save Yente any anxiety which might upset her and her newborn child.

4

Forsaken

WITH THE BIRTH OF ELIZABETH, a more adequate home became an urgent necessity. Benjamin did not earn enough as yet to make this possible, so as soon as Yente regained her strength, Sarah accepted a position with a wealthy Jewish fish merchant as nursemaid to his children.

It was a good position, but it necessitated her living out of town away from Yente. The distance was not terribly great, however, and they arranged to see each other on Sarah's free days.

Yente was left alone. In the few months they had been in London, Benjamin had picked up some English, but Yente had very little opportunity to hear the English language spoken. Yiddish was the predominant language in their neighborhood and certainly in the market down on Petticoat Lane. Sarah had always done most of the purchasing for the family; now Yente had to take over the running of the home. Benjamin continued to work at his trade of cabinetmaking and brought home his meager earnings, barely sufficient for their rent and food.

And then something happened that changed the whole course of their lives. Little Betty was only five weeks old when one night Benjamin did not come home. Yente sat up waiting for him into the wee hours, but still he did not come. She knew nothing about his sister and her designs for him. In the morning she looked about the room, and something told her to go through their few belongings. In the corner of a bureau drawer she found an envelope, which she hastily opened. It was a note in an unfamiliar handwriting. It was from Regina, Benjamin's sister, telling Yente that her husband was on his way back to his father in Poland and that she should forget him. Enclosed were three pound notes ($15.00) for her immediate needs. Yente was stunned. She read and reread the note. No, it could not be true. She must be dreaming. Surely Benjamin would not do such a thing. He loved her and their baby and had promised never to leave them. She refused to believe it.

But the bitter fact was that Benjamin did not come home. Slowly, against her will, Yente had to believe that it must be true. Her heart was torn in agony. The baby whimpered, asking to be fed.

Feverish thoughts raced through her mind. She had to take action, and she knew what she would do. She fed the baby, tidied the room, and dressed herself and her little one. Her face was flushed and her heart beat wildly, but there was determination in her eyes. If Benjamin were on his way to Poland, so must she be. She must get her papers together—her marriage license was all she needed. She looked for it, but that too was gone. Inexperienced and young as she was, she realized that something dreadful had happened. She broke down and cried without restraint.

The most valuable possessions she had were the featherbeds made of goose down that she had brought from Poland. She would sell them, and if that were not enough, she would also sell her wedding ring. Carefully and with a broken heart she took off the ring for the first time since her marriage and put it in her purse.

She asked a neighbor to mind the baby, took her featherbeds under her arms, and made her way to Petticoat Lane, where she was certain she could sell them. Sure enough, a ready buyer came along and offered her the handsome sum of five pounds. To Yente this was a small fortune, even though the down was worth much more. It meant an open door to her husband, the father of her child. She did not stop to think why Benjamin had done this or to rebuke him. She felt that somehow Benjamin's sister must have influenced him and succeeded in sending him home, and she knew she had to go to him.

Robbed

Carefully she placed the five pounds in her purse with the three she already had, put the purse in the pocket on her hip, and hurried home to her baby. Next she would take the baby and go to the railroad station to learn how much the fare would be. If necessary, she would sell her wedding ring to make up the fare. But first she had to find someone to interpret for her in the travel office. Her English was still limited and hard to understand.

With the baby in her arms she arrived at the station. Instinctively she touched her pocket to make sure she had her purse, and, to her horror, she found it was gone. She had been robbed—robbed of all her possessions! She reeled and screamed. People came running. The world seemed to be spinning around, and then she felt strong arms around her and a voice, as if in the distance, asking "Who is she?" People replied, "She says she has been robbed. But robbed of what? She is so young and beautiful. Whose baby is she carrying?" On and on went the questions. And then a husky man dressed in a dark blue suit leaned over and steadied her. She clutched at the man's sleeve frantically and through her tears cried, "It is gone, my purse, all I had, my feathers, my all." He looked at her and could not understand. She was speaking Yiddish. People eagerly interpreted the girl's frantic explanations, and he then understood.

He was a policeman, one of those big, burly, kindly men— a Bobby—whom she and Benjamin had so often admired. What a difference between this policeman and the Russians back home. She was sure he would help her. He would find her purse. How could anybody be so cruel to her and her baby? People took her into the store, turned an empty box upside down, and she sat on it. "Calm yourself," they advised her, "and tell us what happened." Yes, she must be calm, she must be strong, she must clear her mind and tell them of the twofold tragedy that had befallen her.

She told them about her husband. They glanced at the finger of her left hand, and she told them the ring was in the purse that had been stolen. She explained that she had decided to sell everything she had to get back to Benjamin. They asked where her marriage certificate was, and she explained that her husband had taken it with him. The people in the crowd looked at one another and then at her, knowingly.

There was a hushed silence. What a pathetic figure—and such a story. The policeman obtained the translated story and asked if she knew anyone in London. Indeed she did. She had a sister Sarah, but she did not know her address. *Oh, what is happening to me?* she wondered. These people were strangers. How could they understand all that had occurred in such a short time? Even she realized that her story seemed incredible, fantastic. People murmured. It was obvious their credulity was strained to the limit, and their sympathy was ebbing fast. They began to walk away.

Sons of Mercy

Then out of the crowd a man appeared. He talked quickly, heatedly, and asked, "Can we Jews, who call ourselves 'Sons of Mercy,' allow this girl to be stranded with her baby in a strange country? What does it matter whether we believe her story or not? The fact is that she is in distress. I call upon you, every one of you, to rally around her. Isn't she a daughter of Israel in anguish? She needs our help. Have mercy, have pity." His words were like magic. Already he was passing around an old battered hat. The crowd was increasing in size, and excited whispers filled the air as hands were stretched out. They were now willing hands, helping hands. The hat

28

went around and around until it was full, and then the policeman took it and placed his own contribution in it. Many had tears in their eyes.

"Here girl, daughter of Israel, here is your fare. We cannot find the despicable person who robbed you, but we believe you and will see that you join your husband, if indeed you have one."

And then a voice came from the back of the large store. Someone whispered, "It is Mr. Chaim Rosen himself." "Daughter," he said, "did you say you had a sister Sarah who was a nursemaid out of town?" "Yes, yes," she cried excitedly. "Her name is Sarah Glaser." "Come, my child," he said, reaching for her hand. "Your sister is with us in Hyams Park. She told us about you and intended to write to you this week. Come, I will take you to her." A miracle had happened. This was the wealthy fish merchant. The crowd looked on in amazement. The baby began to whimper. The man who started the collection now beamed with satisfaction and triumph.

Yente smiled through her tears. The sun was shining for her again, even through heavy clouds. Soon she would see Sarah, and soon, God willing, she would see Benjamin again. In her heart she uttered a prayer of thanksgiving to God for the care He took of her, and she knew that all would be well again. How generous her Jewish people were—just like in Warsaw, always ready to help one another from the fullness of their hearts. She felt so grateful and proud.

Mr. Rosen was a kind man. He took Yente and her baby to his home to meet Sarah. When they arrived, his family welcomed her as if she were their own daughter. Sarah was both joyful and grateful to have her sister with her and to be able to take care of her needs.

For two months Yente enjoyed the hospitality of this friendly Jewish family. Neither Sarah nor the Rosens would permit her to start the long journey back to Poland until she had fully recovered from her shock and the baby was old enough to travel.

The country home of the Rosen family stood all alone in the woods in beautiful surroundings. They kept their own chickens and a cow. Once again Yente tasted the joy of country life, and although her heart was yearning to be with her husband in Poland, she enjoyed every moment in the peaceful surroundings among kind people.

The Homeward Trek

At the time of the coronation of King Edward VII, Sarah took Yente and the baby back to London to see them off at Charing Cross Station for the trip across the English Channel. The sight of the jubilant, joyful masses shouting and hailing their newly crowned king made the two young women more conscious of their own loneliness and helplessness. The hearts of the sisters were heavy as they parted. Sarah took care of all Yente's needs and provided clothing, some food, and many little things she hoped would insure a comfortable journey. Having no identification papers, not even a birth certificate, Yente and her baby were delayed several times on the way. This was an unforeseen circumstance that caused her to run out of clothing for the baby. Soon all diapers were used, and there were no facilities for washing them. Yente could stand everything—the squalor, the weariness, and the hunger—but she agonized for her poor baby. She nursed her as best she could and was as careful as possible with her meager funds.

Exhausted and weary, she increasingly felt the strain of sitting on hard benches with a three-month-old baby in her arms. Often she went without sleep for whole nights. Soon the German train crew left, and the Russians took over. The trains had been anything but clean, although the Germans did come in once a day to sweep, but the journey through Russian Poland was unbearable. The Russians contended that since she was without papers, Yente and her baby were public charges, and they treated her accordingly. One night during one of the numerous train changes, Yente was hustled into a dark section of the train. Before she realized what was happening, she was pushed into a compartment with the baby and told to sit on the floor. The baby was uncomfortable and irritable, and she was on the verge of tears.

Suddenly out of the darkness in a corner of the compartment someone moved. She was rooted to the spot, and then terrible laughter rang out, the laughter of a maniac. She tried to scream, but no sound would come. She tried to laugh, but she was paralyzed with fear. Again came the laughter, hideous and frightening. Panic gripped her, and she finally screamed. Thumping at the door behind her with one hand, she feverishly groped for the handle. The door was flung open from the other side. In a flash the conductor took in the whole situation. The guard had made a mistake and put her in a compartment with a drunken man. Everyone was distressed and embarrassed. How could such a thing have happened? The conductor was infuriated and very apologetic. He led her into her own compartment and tried to quiet little Elizabeth, who by now was screaming at the top of her voice.

Warm milk was brought for the mother and baby, which calmed their nerves. They brought her warm water to wash the grime off her face and to tidy up her baby. A kind Jewish passenger who was on his way to Warsaw offered to help. Realizing the child's needs, he dashed out at the next station and returned with a clean sheet, which he promptly tore apart to provide the necessary diapers.

The long and tedious journey lasted another six days. Would they ever arrive in Warsaw? They stopped at every little village station, and by now word had been passed from place to place that a young Jewish woman, alone and with a baby in her arms, was on the way. Whole delegations from the towns and villages, often headed by the local rabbis, came to the station to greet the young mother and her child. They comforted her and brought her hot meals and other necessities.

Reunion and Forgiveness

At last they arrived in Warsaw. Yente hardly expected Benjamin to be at the station upon her arrival, but Sarah had cabled him, and there he was waiting for her. He told her he had been meeting every incoming train for six days, his anxiety for the safety of her and their baby increasing from day to day.

Now, thank God, they were united again, and he promised that no one would ever come between them. They were two young people in love, and everything was forgiven and forgotten. Shamefaced, Benjamin told her how his sister had prevailed on him to return and how, in a weak moment, he had given in, but that he had suffered ever since. He had learned a bitter lesson and vowed that never again would any of his relatives influence him in his decisions. And he was true to that vow.

Yente was happy again. At first, her father-in-law grudgingly accepted her, seeing how determined his son was to remain with his wife. But soon admiration and a barely concealed pride became apparent in his attitude toward his daughter-in-law. He felt there was no braver girl in all of Poland to have faced her misfortunes so courageously. The family was reconciled, and Yente's sunny nature did not permit her to bear grudges for long. Peace was restored.

This peace, however, was to be shattered by an awesome discovery that was destined to change their lives and that of generations yet unborn. One day Benjamin came face to face with his Messiah.

Abraham Sitenhof, Benjamin's father, believed in "Yihes."

Mr. and Mrs. Benjamin Sitenhof and Baby Elizabeth (Around 1900).

Left to right: Jack, Mary, Elizabeth (standing), Lydia (the author), Yente Sitenhof, and son Ernest, around the year 1913.

Consulaat Generaal der Nederlanden

(NETHERLAND CONSULATE GENERAL.)

CONSUL GENERAAL.
H. S. J. MAÄS.

12. *Blomfield Street,*

London,

E.C.

N.

ALL LETTERS TO BE ADDRESSED TO THE
CONSUL GENERAL AND NOT TO INDIVIDUALS.

Jené Sietenhoff, née Close, born at
Warsaw in Poland, and temporarily residing
in 91, Lichfield Road, Bow, London, holder of a Russian passport issued by the
Governor of Warsaw on May 17, 1900, which
is too old to be used, intends to travel
from London via Rotterdam to the frontier
station in the Netherlands in order to meet
her children who will arrive there from
Hessen-Cassel, and to return with those
children to England.

The annexed photo is that of Jené
Sietenhoff and her children.

London, March 10, 1915,

The Consul General for the Netherlands,

Yente's traveling document.

5

Benjamin Meets the Messiah

FOR A WHILE the sun shone bright upon the lives of the reunited family. Little Elizabeth was the joy of her father's heart. She resembled him to a striking degree with her dark curly hair and small, regular features. Whenever he had the opportunity he would spend a few minutes admiring her, for she was as beautiful as a doll. When Elizabeth was two, her brother Ernest was born. There was great rejoicing at the birth of a son. Life seemed to be crowned with happiness for Yente. Often she thanked God for all His wondrous love to her. To look up to God with gratitude was as natural for Yente as her sunny "Good morning" to the workmen as they filed into the factory every morning. Many times she took a hot dinner to Benjamin or her father-in-law. The factory was working at full capacity, her father-in-law's business was flourishing, and Yente was the envy of many of the young ladies and young mothers with whom she came in contact.

The only thing that marred her happiness was the poverty in the Jewish ghetto around her. Some of the poorer Jewish people struggled just to eke out a living. It reminded her of her former home, her widowed mother, and her own years of struggle. At such times she clung in a childlike way to Benjamin, fearful that something would come along and destroy the happiness she was experiencing and enjoying.

Benjamin carried on his work in his father's carpenter shop, turning out beautiful pieces of furniture. He was very gifted with his hands and was often called "golden hands." He could do anything with them. There was a skillfulness and sensitivity about them that evoked the admiration of many. Soon the young man, scarcely 20 years old, became the foreman of his father's large factory, and there was no doubt that he would later become a partner and eventually the heir of the prosperous establishment.

But the Lord often works in ways different from human expectations. He had better plans for Benjamin than turning out good furniture. He was to be a fellow worker with the Master Carpenter of Nazareth helping to mold souls through the power of the gospel. But on this peaceful summer day, when a Catholic customer came into the shop, Benjamin had no way of knowing about that.

The customer had a small book with black covers in his hand, and he gave it to the young foreman saying, "Read this. A missionary gave it to me. It seems to be a religious book, but it does not have the approval of my church, so I cannot read it. Perhaps you would like to read it."

That Name

It was a copy of the New Testament in Polish, forbidden not only to the Gentile customer but also to Benjamin, an orthodox Jew. He had heard about the book in a very vague manner ever since childhood. It was connected with the unmentionable name of "that Man." They called Him by the cryptic name "Yeshu," interpreted to mean *May His name and memory be blotted out*. Strange and terrible things concerning "that name" and those who believed in Him came to Benjamin's mind. *These believers are all haters of the Jews*, he thought. In olden days they often put the Jews to the sword. They massacred and persecuted his people, and even now few of them had a kind word for the Jews. All the fearful wrongs, injustices, and degradations his people had suffered were engraved deep into his soul. His was the memory of a persecuted people.

When he thought of "that name," he had visions of crowds in the streets oozing a strange and frightening religious fervor. They carried graven images and painted pictures of a woman with a baby in her arms, and other images representing saints, things that were an abomination to the Jewish mind. The crowds were singing strange songs, the very sound of which made his soul shudder. He knew that whenever such processions passed in the streets, it was the better part of wisdom for Jews to disappear because those who did not were often victims of uncontrollable outbursts of religious zeal and mass psychosis, which usually ended in physical violence.

It was, therefore, no wonder that Benjamin was confused upon receiving the book. And yet he was eager to know more about Him, to understand this personality who had evoked so much passion and faith and seemed to have a limitless sway over the masses. Stealthily he put the book in his pocket, determined to read it in private. In the silence of his own room he began to study the book, expecting to read burning words full of denunciation and hatred for the Jews, but he found nothing of the kind. Instead, it was full of sweetness and beauty. It was the story of one whose life was inexpressibly beautiful and whose death was cruel and undeserved. The more he read, the more he was fascinated by the book.

When he read the Sermon on the Mount, tears welled up in his eyes. It opened up a new world of love, beauty, and holiness unmatched and unsurpassed by anything he had ever read or heard. He went through the Gospels and continued reading the other books of the New Testament, and the Spirit of God began working within his heart. He felt more and more drawn to the amazing man of Nazareth. Surely He was a man of God.

The more he read the New Testament, the more convicted he became of sin in his life and the need of a Messiah. He read and reread it until he became very familiar with its pages. There was no question that he was reading of the true Messiah for whom he had yearned since childhood. This yearning had been inherited from past generations, uncounted and forgotten, which reached back through the centuries and millennia to the dim days of the ancient history of his people.

The Living Dead

For a long time Benjamin wrestled within his heart. He sought light, and the Lord heard his longing. Gradually it dawned upon him with an unshakable conviction that He was, beyond any shadow of doubt, the Messiah, the very Son of God, foretold by the prophets, longed for and prayed for by his ancestors up to the present day. He could do nothing else but accept Him.

This, however, was more easily said than done. What about his father? What about his friends? What would his young wife say? Would they call him a traitor or think he was just plain crazy? They would hound him out of town. They would give him up for dead and sit *shiva* (mourn over him as if he were dead). A candle would be lit in the room; all mirrors would be veiled in black; his father would take off his shoes and sit in his stocking feet on a low footstool with a fixed stare of utter despair that is worse than mourning one who has died. To them he would be a living dead man. No one would dare mention his name to his father or to any of his loved ones. They would deny his existence and act as if they had never had a son or a brother. Even his beloved Yente would forsake him. At this thought he felt a sword thrust at his very heart.

It was a burden so crushing for a young man scarcely out of his boyhood that he felt he could not face it. But then there was the irresistible Christ appealing to him and calling him all the while: "And every one that hath forsaken houses, or brethren, or sisters, or father, or mother, or wife, or children, or lands, for my name's sake, shall receive an hundredfold, and shall inherit everlasting life" (Mt. 19:29). He quoted the words that he had read on a number of occasions in that little black book. But now those words seemed as though they came from the mouth of the one who had been crucified for him. He faced an exciting challenge, but he was full of sadness and pleading. He could not endure it any longer. He would confess Him; he would pay the price, no matter what it might be.

One day Yente noticed that Benjamin had been sitting for hours reading out of the little black book, something he had done many times in recent days, and she wondered what it was that he found so utterly engrossing. She never said a word, however, knowing that one day he would, of his own accord, speak to her about it. To Benjamin, the New Testament was the greatest revelation of his life. He now understood so much that had been a mystery to him before.

After his conversion, Benjamin's life changed, and his family noticed the change. He could not conceal it, for it was too vital a part of his being. He was quieter and more subdued. For months he went about his business with a faraway look in his eyes. People commented on it, and some even thought he was losing interest in the business. Little did they know what had happened in his mind and heart. To him a new world had opened—new light and understanding had entered in. The time came when he could no longer conceal his newfound joy in the Messiah of Israel. After a great inner struggle, he went first to his father to tell him of the great light that had dawned in his life.

I Have Come to Bring a Sword, Not Peace

The worst of Benjamin's fears came true. At first his father thought he had become mentally unbalanced. He tried to talk him out of this "strange delusion." But Benjamin was adamant. He quoted prophecies from the Old Testament, pointing out that they were fulfilled literally in the life of Jesus. They were so numerous and accurate in detail that there was no possibility of mistake. He knew in his heart that Jesus was the one for whom he had always longed. Finally his father gave up arguing, and he gave up Benjamin for lost.

Benjamin would have to leave home soon, and his father Abraham would have to forget that he had ever had an only son upon whom all his hopes for the future were centered. He wished his son were dead rather than have him become a *Meshumed*—an apostate.

With a heavy heart Benjamin went to his wife and tried to convey to her his newfound faith. But Yente—trusting, faithful, understanding Yente—also turned on him. She would not live with a *Meshumed*. He would have to choose between her and his Jesus. If he cared more for Him than for his wife and family, he could have Him, but she would stay in Warsaw with her two babies.

Heavyhearted and burdened with a crushing weight, Benjamin decided to leave his loved ones. Deep in his heart he believed that someday, when their wrath had been fully vented and their tempers were cooled, he might be reconciled to and reunited with his family.

But now he must leave his homeland. And where could a young man go in the infancy of the 20th century but to America, that golden land of opportunity for all men? Yes, that's where he would go.

Soon he was on his way to the land across the ocean. After a night of misery and sleeplessness in the third-class train compartment, he arrived red-eyed, weary, and infinitely sad in the city of Kassel, Germany. He spent about six hours in Kassel waiting for the next train to take him to the port city of Rotterdam. Lonely and discomfited, he decided to visit one of the rabbis of whom he had previously heard, and thus kill the hours of waiting for his connection. On the street he asked a passerby for directions to the rabbi's home. When he arrived at the address he had been given, he soon learned that he was in the home of an evangelist who, by some strange coincidence or predetermination, had the exact same name as the rabbi. This evangelist became to Benjamin what Ananias was to Paul after his experience on the road to Damascus.

6

A Strange Prayer
Strangely Answered

B ENJAMIN WAS SHOWN into Mr. Ludwig Sommer's study, a somber, thickly carpeted, dimly lit room. The atmosphere of the solid brown furniture and book-lined walls embraced him warmly. A hushed quiet seemed to permeate Benjamin's weary body and relax his perturbed soul. The dignity and friendliness in the room beckoned him to enter and be still.

The maid who admitted him to the home said that *Herr Prediger* (Preacher) Sommer would see him in a few minutes. What did that mean? Benjamin did not know much German, but his knowledge of the language was sufficient to understand that this wasn't the home of a rabbi but of a Christian preacher. He had prayed on his arrival at the Kassel Station that the Lord would open up the way for him and make His will plain, and here was the answer already.

"Before they call, I will answer; and while they are yet speaking, I will hear" (Isa. 65:24)—these were words Benjamin had read in the Scriptures recently, and now he was experiencing just that. *What a wonderful Savior to have as a friend,* thought Benjamin, as he sat in the leather chair opposite the large oak desk. *What will the Prediger look like?* he wondered. *Will he be surprised to see a Jew? Will I be welcome?* He wondered what attitude believers in Jesus, other than Roman Catholics, had toward Jewish people. This much was sure in his mind: A true believer in the Jewish Messiah could never hate or persecute a Jewish person. How wonderful it would be to meet such a Gentile Christian.

The door opened, and there stood the Prediger. For a brief moment Benjamin caught his breath. The stately figure in the doorway, dressed in a Prince Albert cutaway with a broad cravat covering his chest, came forward with slow, deliberate steps and a warm smile of greeting on his face. He was a man in his 50s, tall, upright, with a wealth of white hair, and a well-groomed white beard accentuating his aristocratic bearing. But the most distinguishing feature about him was his friendly, twinkling, blue eyes that seemed to speak even before he opened his mouth. To Benjamin, in that brief moment, the Prediger embodied all the outward features of his newly found Messiah, as he visualized Him, and he shook his hand immediately, knowing he had found a friend.

After formally introducing himself, the Prediger asked what he could do for Benjamin. On explaining, as best he could in broken German, how he came to be there and asking to be excused for the error (for which he secretly was thankful), the preacher calmly said, "Benjamin Sitenhof, I have waited for you, yea I have even prayed for you. I perceive you are an Eastern Jew from Poland. I have always yearned for the opportunity to witness to an Israelite such as yourself; and the Lord, in whom I believe, has sent you to me." Benjamin then burst out with the story of his recent conversion. He explained that he too had longed for an opportunity to tell someone who would understand, someone who would rejoice with him. He unburdened his heart amid tears of joy and relief; and this man, whose very presence radiated warmth and comfort, listened enraptured. He opened his arms to him as a father, and for the first time since his conversion, Benjamin knelt to pray and thank God for all His ways and tender mercies.

To Eat or Not To Eat

As they rose to their feet, a lady entered the room. Joyfully the preacher introduced Benjamin to Mrs. Sommer, who welcomed him warmly. Dressed in a black dress with white trim at the neck and cuffs, her face serene and kind, she talked quietly and gently to Benjamin, like a mother to her son. Benjamin was surprised when she invited him to be their guest for the evening meal.

Never in his life had he eaten in the home of a Gentile. Would they serve pork of some kind? Ancient taboos inherited from long-forgotten generations still exerted a powerful influence on his thoughts and feelings. It was easier for Benjamin's soul to accept the Lord Jesus as his Savior than for his stomach to be reconciled with unclean things. Without knowing, his soul was echoing back the feelings of another Jew who followed Christ but who still objected to unclean things. "Lord . . . I have never eaten anything that is common or unclean" (Acts 10:14), cried Peter. In the same way, Benjamin's soul objected to any sudden departure from ancient tradition. Besides, the hour was getting late. On the other hand, he had not had a real meal for many hours—he had been so absorbed that he forgot about food. He looked at his watch. In two hours his train would leave for Rotterdam. Oh, how he longed to tarry here with these loving people. As if reading his thoughts, the preacher suggested that he stay overnight and leave on the same train the next day.

If their dear guest objected to eating meat that was not Kosher, surely *Mutter* (as the Prediger called Mrs. Sommer) would find plenty of other food acceptable to him. Benjamin's misgivings gave way rapidly before this onslaught of great kindness and Christian hospitality, and without further coaxing he readily agreed to stay overnight with his newfound friends.

The meal was a memorable one for Benjamin. It was his first taste of Christian friendship. Never in his life had he experienced such a wealth of sympathy and understanding,

41

and from strangers at that. *What miracles faith in Christ can achieve,* he thought. These people were complete strangers to him, people he had never seen or spoken to before, and yet after only two hours he was talking to them as if he had known them all his life. The tie that bound them together, the bond of the Jewish Messiah, seemed so strong and deep that it blotted out all else, even the fact that he was a Jew from Poland in the home of a German Gentile who had nothing in common with him in the ordinary sense. The deep joy of spiritual oneness and Christian fellowship in the Lord was Benjamin's portion that night. Now he understood the fervor and zeal that only faith in a living Savior could impart. That night he had a strange and wonderful peace in his soul.

By noon the next day it was evident to Benjamin, as well as to the preacher, that he would change his plans and postpone his journey to the States. All that morning Benjamin had been eagerly questioning Prediger Sommer concerning the Scriptures. There was so much that was unclear to him. He wanted it all explained, he wanted to delve deep into the treasures of the Word. And so it was that his newfound friend invited him to stay in his home for a few weeks so that they could study the Scriptures together. Benjamin eagerly accepted the invitation. Nothing else was important to him now; he only wanted to feast on the treasures of the New Testament. And here was God's servant—a man conversant in the Scriptures— who was willing to spend time with him expounding and studying the Word. It seemed too good to be true.

In his great enthusiasm, Benjamin almost forgot he had a wife and two children. He was so in love with his Lord and Savior and anxious to know Him better, that all else was secondary in his thoughts. This zeal and desire stayed with Benjamin for the rest of his life. He always put the Lord first, even though at times the cost was very great.

And so for weeks Benjamin sat at the feet of Prediger Sommer, his great teacher, learning and satisfying his hungry soul. His spiritual growth in those weeks was remarkable. The Sommers had two sons near Benjamin's age, and they soon became fast friends. And always the Prediger would wistfully say, "I prayed for an Israelite, and the Lord sent him to me." Oh, how he loved Israel. Benjamin loved his teacher and looked into his face reverently as he expounded the Scriptures, sometimes scarcely believing that he was anything less than an angel from Heaven.

Call Him Jacob—Letter Follows

Benjamin had written to Yente when he decided to stay with the Sommers, but he received no reply. He wrote again and again, and then one day a telegram came announcing the birth of their third child—a second boy. This brought Benjamin down to earth, as it were. Overjoyed, he wired Yente, "Call him Jacob—letter follows."

He knew that his instructions that his newborn son be called Jacob would greatly please Yente for two reasons. Yente's father, of whom she had a very dim but fond memory, was named Jakob, and she wanted to perpetuate his memory by calling his grandson Jacob. Then, too, the fact that Benjamin was willing to have his son named Jacob, and not some outlandish Gentile-sounding name, was evidence to her that he had not broken with his people and that the bonds of love for his own were in no way affected by his newfound faith in Jesus the Messiah. This stratagem of love was not without success.

There ensued a lively correspondence between Yente and Benjamin, a tug of war—Yente implored Benjamin to return, and Benjamin begged Yente to join him. He tried to convey to her the satisfaction and joy his newfound Messiah had given him. He told her he had just begun to really live and that he wanted to share that life with her. Yente was eager to see Benjamin and show him their new baby. What a lovely, big boy he was, and how she longed for Benjamin to again take his rightful place in the family as the father and breadwinner. She missed him and grieved for him more than anyone could understand, but she kept her sorrow to herself. Somehow she hoped that in time she would win Benjamin back to Judaism.

With that thought in her mind, she one day broached the forbidden subject with her father-in-law. Instead of chiding her, he encouraged Yente to go to Benjamin, alone if necessary, leaving the children with a nurse. But Yente would not hear of it. She would take her three precious children with her wherever she went.

She made her plans, and the day finally arrived when Yente, packed and ready for the journey to Kassel, said her good-byes. She was sorry to leave her father-in-law, whom she had learned to love. She would miss him, and he would be unhappy without her. Her ever-smiling face and dancing blue eyes were a tonic to the old man, even when she teased him and made him hold the baby while she attended to something trivial. He would look at her wistfully and ask, "How long, sweet Yente, how long will you be here to be the sunshine of my life?"

He knew that sooner or later Yente would have to join his son who was lost to him, and in his heart of hearts he hoped that she might be the one to win him back to Judaism. He made sure that Yente and the children were well-clothed and had new linen and bedding to take along, these being the first essentials of a new home. There were down and featherbeds (he bought the best for her), pillows, sheets, and tablecloths. He provided the best luggage he could get, and as a parting gift he presented Yente with a pair of silver candlesticks, making her promise to use them every Friday night at dusk.

Little Elizabeth, now four, and Ernest, two, held tightly to each other's hands while the baby, six weeks old, slept in his mother's arms. Yente had no idea as she entered the Warsaw railway station, accompanied by her father-in-law and other members of the family, that this would be her last glimpse of Warsaw for many years. Little did she know the great change that was about to take place in her life and the years of toil, tears, and suffering that would accompany the change.

Yente Comes to Kassel

Benjamin, overjoyed when he heard that Yente and the children were coming, walked about as if in a dream. He roamed the old part of the town through the narrow, crooked streets, the houses of which dated back to the 17th century, to find a suitable home for his family. With the help and recommendation of the Prediger, he rented a three-room, furnished apartment in the basement of a picturesque gabled house, which he knew would appeal to his wife. The money he had when he arrived in Kassel was carefully budgeted for immediate needs. Prediger Sommer not only preached, he owned a fine religious book store and printing plant that he ran with the help of his sons, and Benjamin was welcome to work there, at least temporarily, to earn his keep. Thus, his dear friend looked after him both spiritually and materially.

Benjamin loved to walk through the beautiful old city and over the old bridge spanning the river Fulda, which meandered through the town. He would stand and gaze into the murky water, dreaming of the time when Yente would stand beside him. As he made his way home through the adjoining park, he wondered how long it would be before she too accepted the Messiah Jesus. He was sure that sooner or later she would see the light and share his new happiness. He prayed earnestly that this might take place soon after her arrival.

The day finally came. It was a warm June afternoon, and Benjamin made his way across the vast *Friedrichsplatz* to the station. The market was in full swing. The neat rows of stalls displayed everything from tempting country butter and eggs to men's and women's clothing. Children darted in and out of the rows. There was luscious fruit, and the tempting aroma of ripe plums greeted his nostrils. He stopped just long enough to buy a pound of cherries, which were irresistible and would make the children happy on their arrival.

The train stopped with a jerk. Yente made her way to the carriage door with Elizabeth holding on to one side of her voluminous skirt and Ernest the other side, while she carried Jacob. Before she even got a glimpse of the platform, Benjamin had seen her and hurried to open the door and help her out with the children. The reunion was warm and hearty. In the warmth of their deep love for one another, the memories of estrangement and misunderstanding melted away like snow in the rays of an April sun. Benjamin looked fondly and with pride on his comely wife and bewildered children, who were all taking in for the first time this strange new world. Yente and Benjamin had so much to tell each other, but that had to wait till later.

The great Friedrich Station awed Yente, and the children clung close to her side as they made their way to the exit. Many elegant, horse-drawn cabs were busy picking up and discharging passengers. It was a fascinating scene that reminded Yente of their arrival in London, England, just four years ago. Having rounded up the luggage, Benjamin proceeded to one of those elegant cabs, and Yente was as thrilled as a child at the prospect of riding through town in such a grand conveyance. The little *droschkes*, with their ironclad wheels rumbling with a deafening roar along the cobbled streets of Warsaw, were no comparison to these fashionable cabs, with rubber tires running smoothly along the well-paved asphalt streets of Kassel. The drivers, in their little derby hats with colored feathers, were a sight to behold. The horses were well-groomed and impatient to be off. At last, having loaded luggage and family, they were on their way.

Yente had not even thought about where they would live. But Benjamin had a surprise for her. They rode through beautiful Koenig Strasse, and Yente felt like a queen on display with her family. When they arrived at their apartment, the modest little home held Yente spellbound. Like a new bride she admired everything, running from one room to the other— her happiness was unbounded. *It takes so little to make Yente happy*, thought Benjamin. What a lovely nature she had. Everything pleased her, and she missed nothing in the apartment. When the children were finally in bed, Benjamin and Yente ate their supper and talked until late into the night. Each had so much to to tell and ask the other, and neither broached the subject of Benjamin's faith that night. They were just happy to be together again. Even on that first day, however, Yente's keen eye noticed a change in Benjamin. He was different. *Tonight,* she told herself, *I will not even try to find out why.* She was tired. She would look at him through different eyes tomorrow. Of one thing she was sure, she had done the right thing in coming to him.

She must have been very tired, for when she awoke it was broad daylight, and for a moment she wondered if she were dreaming. Then it all came back to her—memories of the day before—and she jumped up with a start, remembering that the baby would need attention and Elizabeth and Ernest would be hungry. To her amazement, when she opened the door to the kitchen she found them seated around the table, washed, dressed, and eating breakfast. Benjamin sat beside them, his eyes beaming at his offspring, telling them stories while they ate. There was complete happiness in the scene. Yente was almost sorry she had opened the door, for she did not want to disturb them. What a different man Benjamin was. In Warsaw he would never have done such a thing. How kind and considerate he had become. What a gentle manner he had with the children. What had he read in that little black book to change him so? She dressed hastily, promising herself to watch him carefully all day. After they ate breakfast, Benjamin took Elizabeth and Ernest for a walk.

The Battle for a Soul

While they were gone, Yente took stock of the apartment and thanked God, as always, for His blessing in bringing her and her husband together again. Benjamin had said something at breakfast about how quickly the Lord answers prayer and had added, "How I wish you knew Him too, Yente dear." His words came back to her now. What did he mean? To whom was Benjamin referring? No doubt to "that Man." Could it be possible that Benjamin knew something about Him that she had never heard? She would question him on his return and try to learn more about this mystery that had changed her husband so completely.

Benjamin soon found an opportunity to tell Yente what the Lord Jesus Christ meant to him. He was completely changed— "born again of the Spirit," he said—and he was experiencing a deep joy in the knowledge of his Messiah. Yente listened bewildered, trying to formulate some kind of an answer that would be effective in bringing Benjamin back to the fold of Judaism. But how could she, a woman, stand up to Benjamin who knew the Old Testament and the Talmud so well and could even quote from it, while she could not even open her mouth? In Judaism, religion, the Scriptures, and the Talmud were only for men; women were not well-instructed.

She had been taught to say a few prayers. In the morning, upon arising, she would recite *Moide Ani*—"I thank thee O Lord, O eternal and living King, that thou didst restore my soul to me after a night's rest." She also knew that every Jewish person when in grave danger must exclaim *Shema Israel*—"Hear, O Israel: The LORD our God is one LORD" (Dt. 6:4). Upon hearing this, any ghost or ghoul was sure to vanish. She knew that on Sabbath eves she must kindle the lights, cover her face with both hands, and silently offer a prayer beginning with the words, "O God of Abraham, Isaac, and Jacob." She knew about keeping her food kosher—that she must prepare her meat by soaking it for an hour in water and salting it thickly so that not a drop of blood remained in the meat. She still remembered her Gentile neighbor sneering at her and saying, "You are washing all the goodness out of your meat." But she never paid any attention to her. After all, what does a Gentile woman know about Jewish things?

Yente knew many other things pertaining to the wifely and motherly duties of a true daughter of Israel. She also knew that Christians worshiped images and hated the Jews. How was she—poor, unlearned Yente—to answer the profound arguments from the holy book that seemed to prove that "J" (she would not even mention the name) was the Messiah, after all?

She was dumbfounded. Benjamin kept quoting Isaiah 53 right from their Hebrew Bible, not even from the "little black book," the New Testament. He said if any Jew with an open and unprejudiced mind read that chapter, which was omitted in the synagogues whenever the Old Testament was recited, and then read the circumstances of the birth of Christ in the New Testament, he could not fail to see that Jesus was the promised Messiah whom the Jews rejected but many Gentiles accepted.

These words stayed with Yente. Day after day they rang in her ears, and she could not help linking Benjamin's changed life to this new belief. *If only my father-in-law were here,* she thought, *he could surely give Benjamin the right answers and win him back to Judaism.* Again and again, however, she marveled at Benjamin's calm manner and the joyful way he lived.

The Strange Phenomenon— A Gentile Who Loves the Jew

Benjamin was anxious to introduce Yente to his good friends, Prediger Sommer and his family, about whom he had told her so much. *This is indeed a different world,* thought Yente. They were such refined, cultured people, and yet so modest and kind. They put on no airs, and there was a radiance and peace in them for which Yente longed deep in her heart. The Prediger told her how he and his family loved Israel. "But why," she asked, "when the whole world hates the Jews?" He gently explained that he could not help loving the Jews because he loved the greatest Jew of all, the Messiah Jesus, who was foretold by the Jewish prophets. This was all so new to Yente. She pondered everything in her heart.

Meanwhile, Benjamin kept pointing out that only Jesus is the Messiah of the Jews, and that the prophecies of old become real only when fitted and joined together in one life—His life. Who else but Jesus could be the servant of God spoken of in Isaiah 53? And *Yeshaia* (Isaiah) surely was a good Jewish prophet—not a Gentile, or even a Christian. "Benjamin," said Yente, perplexed, "I am only an unlearned woman, and you are a scholar. I cannot answer your arguments, but I am sure there must be an answer, and I am going to find it. If only your own father were here; he would know what to say to you. But I will find the right answer, come what may."

One day, being unable to find peace, she decided to try and find the Jewish view on the question and made plans to visit the local rabbi and ask him to explain Isaiah 53.

The Rabbi is Annoyed

She called on the rabbi one evening, and he admitted her rather unwillingly. *Rabbis never seem to have time to talk to women,* she thought. They were always absorbed in their world of learning.

She introduced herself and in her natural, frank manner came right to the point. "Rabbi," she said, "I must ask you a very important question. I want you to explain to me the 53rd chapter of Isaiah the prophet. To whom does it refer when it says, 'He is brought as a lamb to the slaughter'?"

The rabbi was stunned. How dare a Jewish woman come to him with such a request. He had expected her to ask one of those perennial questions that rabbis are asked by good, pious Jewish women, such as, What is one to do if a drop of milk is spilled by mistake into the chicken pot? Must she get rid of the chicken, or is there a way whereby the rabbi could circumvent this painful and expensive necessity? Or, perhaps she would ask him some question pertaining to the ritual purity of women. There were so many fine points of the law, and pious women were often perplexed concerning the right, God-pleasing thing to do.

Those religious questions, known as *Shoales*, were commonplace for a rabbi. He was prepared to deal with them swiftly and with final authority for just a trifling consideration. But here was a woman, *Eine Ost Juedin* (a Jewess from Eastern Europe), daring to propound a question that had perplexed the great minds of Jewry from time immemorial. And the dispute was by no means solved. Some said that Isaiah was referring to the Messiah and others that he meant the Jews who were always the inerrant sufferers and victims of the *Goim* (Gentiles). The Christians were making the most of this mysterious and baffling prophecy, claiming that "that Man" was the one of whom the great prophet spoke. And here was a simple woman confronting him with the age-old puzzle. He thought of the old proverb, "A fool can throw a stone into the garden that ten wise men will not be able to remove." He would put her in her place.

He cut her short, ignoring her pleading look. "Woman," he said sternly, "religion is not for the woman but for the man. Go about your household tasks, forget what you have heard, keep your dishes kosher, and look after your children and your husband. That is all that is expected of you." With that, he showed her the door and ushered her out, slamming the door behind her. Yente could scarcely regain her breath. Her mind was in confusion as she stood outside. This was surely not the way to answer a woman's simple question. What had she said? What had she done to so enrage the rabbi? What a difference there was in his manner compared to that of Prediger Sommer, the Gentile. Why wouldn't the rabbi answer a simple question pertaining to the Jewish Scriptures?

Out of the Depths

With tears of humiliation and resentment streaming down her face, she made her way home. In the dark she groped quietly to her door and turned the key in the lock. The children were asleep and Benjamin was at one of the religious meetings he often attended and from which he would return so happy and elated that sometimes she almost caught that joy herself. She went to her bedroom in the dark. And suddenly, for the first time in her life, she felt compelled to fall on her knees and cry out, "Oh God, if Isaiah 53 speaks of the Messiah, and Jesus Christ is the one who fulfills this prophecy, forgive my unbelief and have mercy upon me. Oh God, give me a sign that He indeed is my Messiah. Do not leave me in uncertainty." She cried in the agony of her soul. Yente then heard, as if from afar, a voice and saw an angel filling the dark room with a strange light. And the voice said, "Daughter of Israel, be assured it is the Messiah, Jesus Christ, of whom the prophet speaks. Believe and be saved." Her vision faded, and as she rose from her knees she knew that her spiritual rebirth had taken place in that hour.

7

"Jerusalem" in Hamburg

FOR BENJAMIN, Yente's sudden, miraculous conversion completed his joy. He had not dared to hope, even in the secret places of his heart, that his newfound Messiah could work so quickly. This surely proved to him beyond a shadow of a doubt that through the Messiah Jesus all was possible. To Benjamin, who loved the truth and had diligently sought it, it was painful to think that He who was the truth and had become flesh had been rejected and was still being rejected by Israel. The blindness and prejudice of His Jewish brethren appalled him. When Yente too had rejected the truth, his heart ached, and he cried out to God for the light to shine into her life. He knew that nothing short of a miracle could give Yente the same spiritual experience that had changed his life so completely. And now that very miracle had taken place. Oh, how he praised the Lord!

One day Mr. Sommer told him that a Hebrew-Christian pastor and missionary, Dr. Arnold Frank of Hamburg, would be in Kassel, and he wanted Benjamin to meet him. Benjamin had heard about Dr. Frank who, even in those days, was known as the father of Hebrew Christians in Europe and whose hospital and mission were called "Jerusalem" in the great city of Hamburg. It was there that thousands of Jews from Eastern Europe had discovered Jesus as the Messiah of their fondest hopes and prayers. In the "Jerusalem" of that great city, thousands of Jews found a home when the doors of their ancestral homes were slammed in their faces because they dared confess "that Man" as their Redeemer.

Dr. Frank invited Benjamin and Yente to come to Hamburg for baptism, and so the young couple with their three children were duly baptized by Dr. Frank in the Hamburg *Jerusalemkirche*.

A new life then opened up to them, a life made complete and happy through the knowledge of the Lord Jesus Christ as their Savior. Although they were "babes in Christ" (1 Cor. 3:1), they were healthy babes with a constant hunger for "that food which endureth unto everlasting life" (Jn. 6:27). No wonder they were growing fast in knowledge and in the faith.

Benjamin had an older sister, Dora, who years ago had married a businessman, David Fogel from Odessa in southern Russia, and moved to Westphalia in Germany. As children they had understood each other, and Dora, although older, had always looked upon Benjamin as the pride of the family, the one who knew the Torah and was the "hope" of the family. Her sudden departure for Germany had always puzzled Benjamin. He was anxious to meet her again and tell her his "good news." One day his long-anticipated hope came true. But imagine his amazement when, on entering her home, the first thing upon which his eyes rested was a New Testament text hanging on the wall. He read, "Then spoke Jesus again unto them, saying, I am the light of the world" (Jn. 8:12; 9:5). Puzzled, he asked his sister the meaning of that verse in her home. And then the story came out.

Vision on the Mount of Olives

Many years before, Aaron Fogel, a Jewish merchant in Odessa and the father of David, Benjamin's brother-in-law, had come under the spell of a remarkable man named Joseph Rabbinowitz, a prominent lawyer and Jewish leader in Bessarabia in southern Russia.

It was at the time when suffering drove many Jews to desperation and a frantic search for refuge. Jewish blood was flowing freely in the streets of Kishineff, the home of Rabbinowitz.

Burdened with the plight of his people, Rabbinowitz went to Palestine to learn if there were any prospects for establishing a colony there for his persecuted brothers in Russia. When he arrived in Jerusalem, he was shocked to see the sad condition, both materially and spiritually, of the Jews whom he met there. They were mostly old people who had come to die in the Holy Land—not to live. They were disheartened, without hope and vision, living on charity sent to them by pious Jews in Europe, or peddling on the streets of Jerusalem.

The land was devastated, lifeless, and poverty-stricken beyond description. No, Palestine at that time did not look like a solution for the Jewish tragedy. Disheartened and discouraged, Rabbinowitz decided to return home and tell his people to look elsewhere for shelter, since the time for their return to Palestine had not yet come. "In all probability," he told them, "you will have to wait until the Messiah comes, and who knows when that might happen—perhaps today, perhaps tomorrow, in a year, or, perish the thought, never at all!"

Heavyhearted, he decided to walk up the slopes of the Mount of Olives to catch a last glimpse of Jerusalem, so precious, so desirable to those in exile in far-flung lands, but so disappointing when encountered face to face.

In silent meditation, he sat down on a stone. In his mind he quickly reviewed the history of his people—the call of Abraham, God's promises to him and to his children; Egypt and the oppression there; then back to the land again, led by the mighty hand of God through Moses in God's grace and bounty; disobedience and rebellion on the part of his people; prophets and seers, kings and leaders sent by God, only to be disobeyed and rejected; and that Man of Nazareth, of whom he had once read secretly in a little Hebrew Testament. Those amazing words had never escaped him, "O Jerusalem, Jerusalem, thou that killest the prophets, and stonest them who are sent unto thee, how often would I have gathered thy children together, even as a hen gathereth her chickens under her wings, and ye would not!" (Mt. 23:37).

In a moment of sudden illumination, like the prophets of old, an inexorable conviction came to him: The key to the Holy Land and the future of Israel is in the hands of our Brother, Jesus!

This sudden persuasion shook Joseph Rabbinowitz to the very core of his being. With this thought burning in his soul, he went back to his native Bessarabia, and, with flaming words borne on the wings of a great faith and enthusiasm, he preached Jesus, Israel's Messiah and Savior. He continued to identify himself with the Jewish people and saw the need of bringing Christ into the Jewish synagogue, home, and street.

As a result of his fiery testimony, his own wife and seven children, as well as hundreds of other Jews of his own city and in neighboring Odessa and many other towns and villages, accepted Christ. Thousands of Jews in southern Russia were, for the first time in their lives, compelled to give serious thought to the claims of the messiahship of their Brother, Jesus.

Aaron Fogel was among the firstfruits of Rabbinowitz's labor. When his son David married Dora Sitenhof, neither of them were as yet believers in Jesus. Soon they left for Germany, where they established themselves in business. But then Father Aaron arrived from Russia to visit the young couple. He was so full of his great Savior and the wonderful gospel he had heard that soon both David and Dora accepted Jesus as their Lord. This happened around the year 1900.

Thus, God amazingly led brother and sister, by different ways, one in Poland and the other in Germany, to find Christ; and in finding Him, they also found one another.

In the few years since the conversion of David and his family, he had preached the gospel to Jew and Gentile alike, using every available hour to witness for his Savior. David was a very successful businessman, a man of character and resolve. He was highly respected both in the community and at the chapel where the family worshiped. He was also a man of rigid discipline and courageous action. He was zealous for the faith and preached Christ whenever possible. His vacations were invariably spent conducting evangelistic services in different parts of Germany. Dora was small of stature but possessed a great heart and a loving and gentle nature and was a ministering angel to all who knew her.

Salesman for the Lord

The evening before Benjamin's departure, he confided in his sister and brother-in-law his great longing and aspiration to be called of the Lord to be a full-time missionary to his own people. That was his goal, and he told them that all his strivings would be to that end. David promised to try to help him achieve his aim. "In the meantime," he said, "let us work together and grow together." Benjamin did not understand what David meant until he told him his plan. David asked Benjamin to travel for his company, and while visiting all the important cities of Germany, he would have opportunities to witness for the Lord. This appealed to Benjamin immediately, and he arranged to start at once.

What a surprise for Yente when Benjamin returned to Kassel with the news of the conversion of David and Dora and a new, shiny, black bag containing samples for his new position. Benjamin, a salesman? Benjamin was a craftsman, a master cabinetmaker, but no salesman! Yente knew that, but, sensing his enthusiasm, she said nothing and rejoiced with him. She had great faith, and even as a young believer she knew that God could make of Benjamin what He wanted him to be. Her love for her newfound Messiah was unbounded, and together they were happy in the assurance that they could endure all things.

Little did they know how soon they would experience the "valley of the shadow."

8

The Beauty of Holiness

WHEN THEIR FOURTH CHILD, a beautiful little girl, came along, they named her Marie Hannah after their good friend, Mrs. Sommer, whom they thought of as their spiritual mother. To the Sommers, Benjamin, Yente, and their children were as precious as their own, and the two families spent every holiday and season of rejoicing together at the Sommers' home in the beautiful suburb of Wilhelmshoehe.

Here Benjamin saw the treasure of the Christian life displayed in all its loveliness. Here he learned the beauty of daily family devotions. Here he had an example of the spiritual riches that await the believer when he dedicates his life wholly to the Lord. How he longed to do just that.

Together the two families went to the beautiful park in Wilhelmshoehe. Together they climbed the white stone steps leading to the crystal clear fountains and ponds beneath the monument containing large goldfish, much to the delight of the children. This was their favorite outing.

On public holidays when there were crowds gathered to enjoy the beauty of the scenery and to inhale the fragrance of the tall, age-old trees, Benjamin would produce a batch of tracts and distribute them to the crowd. On many occasions he entered into conversations with individuals, explaining to them the way of salvation. Benjamin was happy at such times. It was in the park that he had his very first experiences as a witness for His Master. He often joined some of the other brethren and took part in open-air meetings. Thus, he grew in the knowledge of the Lord and the Scriptures.

The prayer meetings held at the chapel twice a week were faithfully attended by Benjamin; and whenever Yente could leave the children asleep, she too would creep out and join him there.

A Dreaded Disease

Yente tried as much as possible to relieve Benjamin of family problems and burdens. She could see that his work was taxing his strength, and he was beginning to look wan and thin. In her heart she was filled with anxiety that he would become ill. Yente was not the only one who had noticed Benjamin's pale face; Brother Sommer was also aware that Benjamin's health was not as good as before. He mentioned this to Dr. Schmidt, a believer who was keenly interested in the Sitenhof family.

One evening after prayer meeting Dr. Schmidt approached Benjamin and made an appointment to see him the next day. It was discovered that one of Benjamin's lungs was seriously affected by the dreaded tuberculosis and that immediate treatment at a sanatorium was imperative.

In the early years of the century, tuberculosis was a sinister disease whose victims seldom escaped without paying the supreme penalty. There were no medicines such as penicillin or streptomycin or any of the life-saving mediums available today. Early discovery of the malady, good nourishment, and fresh air were the only hope of those afflicted with the disease.

Yente tried to be brave at this sudden turn of events. Before her conversion she would probably have broken down under the impact of the bad news, but now she bore up valiantly. She carried her burden to the Lord in prayer daily, drawing strength from the fountain of living water. David was notified immediately, and after consultation with the doctor, he arranged for Benjamin to go to the sanatorium at Liebspringen in the Rhineland, famed for beneficial results in similar cases. It was hoped that there the disease would be checked.

And so it came about in February 1908 that David found a small home for Yente in the city of Biebrich am Rhein where she could be near Benjamin, realizing that it might be months or even a year before he would be discharged.

David was like a father to Yente and her children. He lost no time and did not count the cost in getting them settled. Although he had two children of his own, he divided his time between taking care of his own family and Yente's family.

As for Yente, she was at her best in times of trial. Hidden resources of strength, courage, and faith welled up in her when the storms of life seemed ready to overwhelm her. Now added to her natural qualities of spirit was her strong faith in her wonderful Messiah, who had promised never to leave or forsake her.

A Woman of Valor

Yente, always full of initiative, knew that she could not leave the whole burden of her family on David's shoulders, so she began to look for suitable employment that she could do in her home to help feed her children. On some days she took in sewing, alterations, and similar work. At other times she left the two older children in school and the two younger ones with a neighbor and did housework at the home of a Christian friend.

She found a chapel to which she attached herself at once, for to Yente spiritual food was as important as physical food. Somehow, in spite of her burdens and many duties, she managed to attend at least the prayer meetings after putting the children to bed. Her Christian friends tried to help her. They were impressed with the courage and determination of this Jewess who loved her Lord with a zeal that put some of them to shame. She worked day and night to keep her children clean and well-fed—and she was expecting yet another child.

Benjamin's heart was heavy when he was first told of his condition. *Who will take care of my little flock?* he pondered. But seeing the way Yente took charge and observing her courage and faith, his faith was strengthened. He allowed the Lord to take over, and he responded favorably to the treatment. After the first few months, hope for a complete recovery was beckoning.

Yente's days were filled to the brim with activity. She washed, shopped, cooked, and ironed for her own family—and then she did the same for others. She seemed to have superhuman strength. She was 26 years old but looked younger. The Lord's favor was plainly written in her lovely face. Buffeted by angry waves, she remained calm and serene, mistress of her boat and its precious little crew, their course set by the star of hope.

A Stranger at the Door

One evening after she had put the children to bed and was mending clothes, there was a timid knock at her door. At first she thought she had imagined it, for who would be coming to see her at that time of night? It was 8:30, and she knew of no one who might call on her that evening. However, on hearing the knock a second time she went to the door and, as was her habit, peered through the small peephole in the door to see who was there. Without opening the door, she saw a bearded man of medium stature and asked who it was.

A pair of tired eyes met hers. Then came the reply, not in German but in Russian, "Please open the door." She opened the door without another thought and asked the stranger to enter. "Who are you?" she demanded. "From where have you come?" He sat down and breathed heavily. "My name is Herman Berg," he explained, "and I come from the city of Kiev in the Ukraine."

Then he unfolded a story of woe, very much the same as the suffering and tragedy common among the Jews of Czarist Russia. Unable to stand the gross injustice and persecution of his people, he had joined an underground movement against the Czar. Then he was caught and pressed into the service of the Czar as a soldier. But in the Russian army his lot was even worse. Apart from the hardship of being a Russian soldier, he was singled out for special ridicule as a Jew.

Nothing he did satisfied those over him. "Jew, Jew," was the derisive cry that followed him wherever he went. He decided to run away from Russia, even though his heart was breaking for his wife and two children whom he had to leave behind. But what chance would he or his family have if he stayed on? Abroad he might be able to improve his position and eventually deliver his wife and children from the plight of the Jews in Russia.

And so he made his way across the border, risking imprisonment in Siberia. Eventually he arrived in Kassel. This evening when he came out of the railroad station bewildered and in need of a place to go, Herr Maximilian, a cab driver waiting for a passenger, noticed the strange and confused Jew and directed him to Frau Sitenhof. And here he was. Yente knew Max, as they called him in the chapel, for he was a Christian and highly respected among the brethren.

The stranger could speak no German, but she noticed that he was a man of refinement and culture. He was about 30 years old and well-spoken. His face was kind, though sad, and his small black beard and friendly eyes made a favorable impression.

He told her he was an experienced mechanic and was sure he could earn a living if he could get a job repairing sewing machines and things like that.

But what was Yente to do? How could she, herself so badly in need, help put a roof over his head? He could not even speak the German language, and she was a lonely woman with young children. Something must be done, and fast, for the evening was already far spent. The first need was a place for the weary wanderer to rest his head. As for the future, she would talk to her Lord in the stillness of the night and ask Him for guidance.

She briefly told Mr. Berg about herself and her situation. She explained that her husband was in a sanatorium, sick with tuberculosis, and that they had young children. "Nevertheless," she ended cheerfully, "I have a source of comfort and support of which you know nothing." And then she told him of the Messiah of Israel and how she had learned to lean heavily on Him regardless of the difficulties and problems.

He listened intently without a word, and when she finished he said, "I too need a fountain from which I can draw strength, wisdom, and comfort. Will you please tell me more about it tomorrow?"

Herman Berg spent that night at the Salvation Army shelter to which Yente directed him. Yielded completely to His will, the Lord was willing to use her to help this lost soul.

Bright and early the next morning he turned up at her home. He looked like a different man, rested and clear-eyed. Yente found a room for him nearby, and then they surveyed the situation together. She promised to help him, for he needed her to interpret for him. In the evening they went to prayer meeting at the chapel, and although Mr. Berg could not understand what was said, the quiet hour of meditation and reverence impressed him more than anything else. He was grateful when Yente translated for him.

Gentiles with a Difference

Never in his life had he met such strange people. True, they were Gentiles, but they were so different from the ones he knew back in Russia.

> Oi, Oi, Oi
> Drunk is a goy (Gentile)
> Drunk is he and drink must he
> 'Cause he is a goy.

With these words the Jewish boys and girls mocked the drunkenness and debauchery of the Russian Gentiles. It gave them a little taste of vengeance and a pleasing sense of their

Lowenburg Castle in Kassel.—Wilhelms Hoehe

Lydia—Sweet Sixteen

Victor at twenty-two

Front row: Bride and groom,
Lydia and Victor Buksbazen.
Back: Lydia's parents,
Yente and Benjamin Sitenhof.

Yente was fond of her grandson
John, Lydia's firstborn.

Yente and Benjamin befriending
a refugee boy from Germany.

The author's sons at ages seven
and eleven: Victor, Jr.,
and John David.

own superiority. But these people, although Gentiles, were different. They were reverent, meditative, and possessed a peace and serenity that appealed to him greatly. *Could it be,* he mused, *that the Jesus of whom Mrs. Sitenhof spoke has something to do with their strange behavior?*

Yente's First Trophy

Yente introduced Herman to the brethren, and Max assured her that he would help him find a job or part-time work. There were others who were eager to help, and prayer was offered for this lonely Jew who had been thrust in their midst and who was so anxious to understand all that happened.

Weeks went by, but because he could not speak German, Herman could find no work. Yente urged him to learn German, for although she herself did not speak it well, she had learned to read and understand it perfectly.

She read the Bible with Herman, while Max instructed him in Yente's home, and not only did he learn the German language, he also learned God's language and God's plan for his life. Soon the day came when he accepted Jesus as his Messiah and Lord.

Near the end of July, when Yente could do no outside work since she was expecting her fifth child early in August, Herman told her of his decision for Christ. He had visited Benjamin at the sanatorium on several occasions, and he and Benjamin had had earnest conversations regarding the Messiah of Israel. Yente's testimony and Benjamin's complete faith puzzled him at first, but he soon realized that it could only be the power of a living God that was sustaining them through all their trials, and he longed for the same assurance and peace. When he accepted the Lord, Herman too experienced that new surge of life and hope that is given to every believer.

Soon after his conversion he found odd jobs, and he performed them well. He repaired bicycles and sewing machines, saving every *pfennig* for the fare to send to his wife and children, who were eagerly waiting to join him. Yente helped him in every way possible, sharing her last crust of bread with him.

Lydia

Soon the time arrived when it was Mr. Berg's turn to help Yente. She gave birth to a baby girl, and he looked after the other children.

David came the day after the baby was born, bringing gifts of food and clothing for all.

Yente pondered over a name for the new baby. She opened her Bible to Acts 16, and her eyes fell upon verses 14 and 15:

> And a certain woman, named Lydia, a seller of purple, of the city of Thyatira, who worshiped God, heard us; whose heart the Lord opened, that she attended unto the things which were spoken by Paul. And when she was baptized, and her household, she besought us, saying, If ye have judged me to be faithful to the Lord, come into my house, and abide there. And she constrained us.

Ah, Lydia, she thought. *That's a beautiful name. I will call my child Lydia, and may she be faithful to the Lord and as willing to love and serve His brethren as was her namesake.*

9

The Steep and Winding Path

YENTE'S STAMINA WAS REMARKABLE. On the third day after Lydia's birth she was up and about—singing, cooking, washing, and cleaning—so active that her German neighbors, who could scarcely believe their ears, came to see this unusual woman who cared so little for herself but so much for the things of God.

She seemed never to tire of "preaching" to them, and yet they could not resent her, for although handicapped by her husband's sickness and with insufficient food for her little ones, to say nothing of herself, she always smiled and went about with a song on her lips and in her heart. Her neighbors marveled. "How could a woman recuperate so quickly?" they asked one another. "It took most of us about two weeks to recover after our children were born. She must have the strength of a Russian Cossack," they concluded. They could not help admiring her, and some of them even offered to help care for her children now and then. Poverty was nothing new in the neighborhood where Yente lived. No one could boast of an abundance of this world's goods, yet none was so devoid of basic necessities as was Yente. "This Jewish woman has courage," they all agreed.

Benjamin Recovers

At last, after long months of waiting and hoping, Benjamin was well enough to leave the sanatorium. A family conclave was held in which David Fogel, Preacher Sommer, and the newfound friend in need, Herman Berg, took part. They concluded that the best thing for Benjamin and Yente would be to move back to Kassel where many Christian friends would welcome them. Herman also decided to cast in his lot with the Sitenhofs.

And so, early in 1909, they began the trek back. Wistfully Yente sighed and wondered, *Shall I ever find a place I can really call home?*

She was only 26 but was already the mother of five children, and her life thus far had been a constant wandering and pilgrimage to unknown and uncharted places. Out of a longing heart came a song she had recently heard in the Brethren Fellowship: "Where shall the soul find the haven of rest?" But out of the depths of her being the answer came. *Yente, you have been a pilgrim all your life, but in all your wanderings your God led you step by step and walked with you all along the steep path.*

Yente was satisfied that God was leading, and she knew she must follow.

Benjamin, although still wan and delicate, was improving all the time, but his doctor advised him to go slowly and not exhaust himself by long hours of work. He continued to grow stronger day by day, and in due course he took up the burden of breadwinner again. His talents as a cabinetmaker and builder placed him in good stead. His right hand did not forget its cunning during the period of enforced idleness.

Another Reunion

Herman Berg eventually saved enough money to bring his family from Russia. Finally the day came when the little home, which Yente helped to prepare for the new arrivals, was ready to receive them. Yente thought of everything, even a vase of flowers on the table.

Herman was anxious to tell his wife about the Messiah right after her arrival. He prayed fervently that this news would not be too shocking for her.

It was a happy party that met the Berg family at the station, and soon they were at home celebrating the joyful occasion with coffee and cake. At last Herman's prayer had been answered, and his loved ones were with him in Germany. At the table he thanked God for this. Not accustomed to such prayer, his wife was so shocked that she sat in ponderous silence for the rest of the evening, wondering what had happened to her husband. Herman, however, appeared unconcerned. *Oh that he might always be as strong in the Lord as he is today,* thought Yente and Benjamin.

In spite of his physical weakness, Benjamin tried valiantly to provide his family with food and shelter. One of his lungs had been permanently sealed, and any strain taxed him. Yet he was able to pursue his occupation, and with care and rest, which Yente encouraged, his health gradually improved.

The three years from 1909 to 1911 were happy ones of family life and Christian fellowship, of physical growth for the children and spiritual maturity for their parents. Benjamin, however, was becoming burdened for service on the mission field, and especially for his own people, the Jews. This thought was with him day and night. The desire to go into full-time service for the Lord gripped him to such an extent that he and Yente had regular prayer sessions, imploring the Lord that if it were His will, He would make the way clear and send him.

The Call to Argentina

One day several missionaries, natives of Kassel, came home on furlough. Benjamin confided his earnest desire to these men and asked their advice concerning South America. He was told that there was an increasing Jewish population on that distant continent, especially in Argentina, and they were in great need of the gospel. Who could better present it to them than a Hebrew Christian—one of their own flesh and blood?

To Benjamin this was a clear indication that Argentina was the land where the Lord wanted him to go as His messenger. With this in view, he took an intensive course of Bible study.

Then one day Benjamin received an invitation from a group of Brethren in Argentina who were deeply concerned by the lack of a Christian testimony to Israel in their midst. They had heard about this young brother and wanted him to come. But would he be willing to come alone at first and bring his family later?

Initially the idea of going alone did not appeal to him. How could he leave Yente with five children, the youngest three years of age, to fend for themselves, even if only for a short while? No, he could not do that. And yet, the more he thought about it, the more convinced he became that it was the Lord's will for him and that the Lord would provide for his family during his absence.

Of course he would be going out on faith, and that meant being left with no income at all. The amazing thing was that Yente encouraged him to go. She had observed him closely and knew that if he missed this opportunity, it would make him very unhappy. Benjamin planned to work part time at his well-paying trade in Buenos Aires, hoping to send for his family in a very short time.

But Yente had already made plans to work herself and provide for the children. It would give Benjamin time to settle down, complete the course of Bible studies in South America, and prepare a home for her and their little ones when they could join him.

The Departure

It was a chilly November day when Benjamin departed for South America. Yente had been busy packing his luggage. She went about her daily chores with a resolute expression on her face. Now and then she told the children in a subdued voice that daddy was about to leave on a long journey and that they should be especially good. The children played house until dusk, then gathered around the old pieces of luggage, whispering to one another. Their faces were eager as they made their own plans for their journey across the big ocean. Mother had told them that in a very short time they too would follow their daddy.

Upstairs in the big bedroom, Yente opened every drawer and closet to see if she had forgotten anything that might be useful for Benjamin on the long journey. There was the warm scarf that David had sent him for Christmas, which she had kept aside. She drew it out of its hiding place and looked at it lovingly with tears streaming down her cheeks.

She knew she had to show a brave face to the children; she must not let them know how her heart ached. She was determined that Benjamin should go alone, and, if it were God's will, she would follow with the children. But deep down in her heart she had a sense of foreboding. Benjamin was not strong. He had never been the same since his sanatorium days. The cough had not left him entirely, and she was afraid of how the hot climate in Argentina would affect his health.

Somehow she could not help feeling that she would not see Benjamin for a long, long time. She knew she would have to be the breadwinner for her five children, and she always thought of the attitude of the German people and that, in spite of everything, she was a foreigner in a foreign land. Her many Christian friends, who loved her as their own, had promised Benjamin they would take care of her. But she knew a feeling of loneliness, even in Christian circles, when careless words and looks seemed to say, "What are you, a Jewess, doing here among us good German Christians?" Even the faith that should have bound them together and made them one did not always overcome the long-ingrained inhibitions and deep-rooted mistrust.

She went downstairs with a heavy heart, busied herself about the kitchen, prepared supper, washed the children one by one (as was her usual, methodical practice), and brushed the girls' hair, all the while not saying a word. But the tension in her expression revealed her innermost thoughts. Here she was, barely 29 years of age, alone in a strange country with five children looking to her for food, shelter, and comfort. But she knew the Lord would strengthen her. Her prayers would go up morning and night. She had complete faith. She had experienced His wonderful power all these years since her conversion, and she knew He would not fail her now.

The table was laid, and the children sat down quietly in an atmosphere of expectancy. As they ate, they looked at one another with large, sad eyes, wondering what was going to happen next. Toward the end of the meal there was a sound of footsteps on the path outside. The front door opened hastily, and Benjamin came in. As he entered the room he whispered something to Yente, and, as if they had rehearsed their parts, both made ready to say good-bye. The kerosene lamp on the table shed an uncanny glow, emphasizing the shadows in the far corners of the room. Nothing seemed to have changed, and yet to Yente everything had changed. It was as if she were set adrift in a boat in the middle of the ocean without a compass. There was no time to be lost. Benjamin whispered to her that he did not wish her to accompany him.

With an expression of utter sadness on his face, Benjamin went to each child in turn, gave each a hurried kiss, embraced Yente for one brief moment, took his black hat, picked up his small bags, and was gone. The children sat in their places motionless. Yente came and took her place beside them, and as if by mutual silent agreement, they buried their heads in their hands. The owl in the arbor outside called its night cry— as usual. Or was there an added tone of haunting sadness this evening? Could it be true that they had been left alone?

10

A Hard School

THE NEWS QUICKLY SPREAD among friends that Benjamin Sitenhof had left for the mission field. It was a surprise. They would have liked to have given him a real send-off, but Yente explained that he had managed to secure passage at the last moment and had hurried his departure, not knowing when another opportunity might be available. Only a small group of friends came to a special prayer meeting conducted by Pastor Sommer, committing Benjamin to God for his distant voyage and future work.

Alone and with a family of five growing children, Yente made plans to keep the wolf from the door. She was determined that while there was breath in her and the good Lord above, her children would not suffer want. She would carry on until the day when they were able to join Benjamin in Argentina.

Frau Emma Schmidt, the farmer's wife, had promised her the early morning delivery of butter, eggs, and apples to sell. Each day at 4 a.m. she hurried to the station to collect the produce so that she might be the first at the market. When she had sold everything, she ran home to give the children their breakfast, and by 8 a.m. they were off to school and kindergarten. Then she hurried along to do the housecleaning in a private home and was back by 2 p.m., just in time to collect the large lamb's wool sacks—she mended a stack every week. After three hours of work at the sacks, she cooked a good meal for the children, delivered her sacks after supper, got the children off to bed, and then did her own housework. A woman had asked Yente to do her washing if she could spare the time, and on top of all this, an insurance company asked her to clean their offices from 3 to 4 a.m.

Elizabeth was 11 years old and a great help to her mother with the younger children. She brought them home from school and took care of them like a little mother. Elizabeth was dependable, a really good child—bless her. Yente's heart flooded with warmth as she thought of her and her other children—the poor little *pigeons*.

Her thoughts were interrupted by Lydia who was rubbing her eyes and crying that she wanted to go to bed. Elizabeth came to her mother's chair and, stroking her hair, whispered that she would put the children to bed and let her mother rest. The two boys demurred a little, but after their elder sister gave them a stern look, they scampered off to bed.

The Cottage with the Red Roof and the *Laube*

By the time Yente got word from Benjamin that he had arrived safely in Buenos Aires, she had so organized her life that her children lacked for nothing. They lived in a little, red-roofed cottage that, along with others like it, formed a crescent around an open courtyard with a little green yard in the center, the "green pastures" of all the residents, especially their children and dogs. Their cottage was the last one in the row and ended at a high wall dividing their street from the next.

Outside the little home was an arbor with a roof fixed to the high wall and overgrown with ivy. They called it the *laube* in German. It was Yente's favorite spot. There she gathered the children whenever she had a moment to spare, told them Bible stories, and made plans for the time when they would join their father. The laube was the pride and joy of the family, and Elizabeth often played house there with the younger children. The laube was the children's own *house* in a special way, and many happy hours were spent there.

All This and Cake Too

The boys—Ernest, nine, and Jacob, seven—delighted in climbing up the sides of the trellis to see who could reach the top first, and screams of delight were heard from the winner. Here the children invariably gathered around their mother when she came home from her day's work with the *surprise*, for Yente somehow always managed to procure a surprise for her brood, be it ever so small. Sometimes it was a small bar of chocolate or a broken crumb cake bought from the baker at a greatly reduced price. Sometimes it was hard candy. But always there was something to make their hearts glad.

The crumb cake, broken doughnuts, or sometimes simply cake crumbs were the most popular with the children. Moved by sympathy for the hardworking mother and her children, a young woman at the bakery shop saved all the broken cakes and cookies, filled a bag, and, as Yente passed the shop at night, beckoned to her and let her have the bag for ten *pfenning*. Sometimes it was a very large bag. Yente suspected that this kind soul, who knew her circumstances, broke the cakes purposely so that she could let her have them for such a small price. So Yente's children had cake too.

People are very kind to us, Yente thought. Although she worked hard, she felt that strength was flowing into her being from a secret well of energy. Her home was spotless, her children were clean and nourished, and their clothing was mended. She was a Jewess who was watched with scrutinizing eyes by everyone, and she felt she should not invite any unfavorable comments, especially among the painstakingly clean German housewives. She was obsessed with a fear that if she lowered her standards of cleanliness, she might be referred to as *Die Schmutzige Juedin*.

The two older children went to school and the three younger ones to kindergarten, thus giving Yente most of the day to do outside work. She went from one job to another, keeping strictly to her schedule every day. By the time she reached home, cooked a meal, and got the children to bed (with Elizabeth's help), she felt weary.

The spring and summer months were much easier, for then she had fruit to sell at the market and did less housecleaning for other people. The German people were very exacting, but she measured up to their neat standards. She even found time to make the children's clothing, including sailor suits for the boys. The neighbors marveled when, on Sunday mornings, the Sitenhof children appeared all fresh and clean, the girls in starched and ironed dresses, and the boys in spic-and-span suits.

But winter proved to be a great strain on Yente. Doing large family washes by hand in damp cellars and rinsing them in three or four changes of icy cold water told on her in time. Her skirt often froze and looked like a hoop by the time she got home. She would *defrost* it in the warm kitchen, to the delight of the children—but to the damaging of her health. Gradually she developed rheumatism and had to give up doing the big washes. In their place she took a job cleaning law offices, which necessitated her getting up at 4 a.m. and waxing and polishing floors on her knees for two hours or more.

A Pilgrim in a Foreign Land

Benjamin, in the meantime, was trying to get established in Argentina. The group of Christians in Buenos Aires welcomed him warmly, rejoicing that at last their prayers had been answered and a messenger had been sent to bear a Christian witness to the ever-growing Jewish community. Benjamin gave himself wholeheartedly to his work. There were so many poor and wretched people in that great metropolis, a city of vice and degradation. His heart ached for these souls adrift. Some of them were carried away from their homes by cunning and deceit.

To many disillusioned and heartbroken souls, Benjamin was not only a link with their old homes in Europe but a harbinger of hope. In his spare time he worked at completing a course of Bible study that would qualify him for full-time service in the gospel.

Friends rallied around, and now and then he was even able to send some money to his family. This, however, seldom reached Yente, since the mails were pilfered frequently in those days. But Yente wrote him encouraging letters, telling him only of the bright events in their lives and keeping to herself the burdens she carried and the sacrifices she had to endure to keep a roof over their heads and the wolf away from the door. She told him that she was being encouraged by the brethren, especially Prediger Sommer, and that they looked forward to a reunion soon. They even discussed at the prayer meetings the question of sending Yente and her children to Buenos Aires, so that the family could be together. But the funds for the fare for six could not be raised, and the months and years went by in an endless struggle for Yente.

Benjamin wrote that the hot, humid climate was exacting a heavy toll on his frail health. He had to be hospitalized for a few months in 1913, and it seemed that it might be wise for him to return to Germany. But he had no money for the journey, and so he decided to work and save for his fare.

In a Princely Home

In the spring of 1913 Yente met a servant of God who helped her in a marvelous way. The law offices where she worked had changed their cleaning schedule. Much to Yente's relief, she was able to do her work from 3 to 5 p.m. One day Yente arrived at work a little early and, on entering the offices, noticed a tall, military-looking man in conference with one of the attorneys.

This attorney had taken an interest in Yente and had questioned her on several occasions about herself and her circumstances. He told her he thought she looked too refined to be doing such hard work, and he sometimes wondered if it were not too much for her. She told him about herself and Benjamin, and he promised to help her find less exhausting work.

Now he called her in and introduced her to his client, a major who was an aide to the princely House of Hesse. He explained that there was a vacancy for a chambermaid at the princess' winter residence, and he had recommended her for the job, which was easy and paid well. Yente could scarcely believe her ears. Could it be that she, a foreigner, could even enter the household of the princess? Yente was modest, and in her humble way she gave voice to her thoughts. "Say little and work well," the major advised her, "and you have the job." Thanking her would-be employer with tears in her eyes, she ran home as if on air. Gathering her five children about her, she thanked her Heavenly Father who cared for them even more than she knew or expected.

Her hours were to be from 9:30 a.m. to 3 p.m. After a week of special instruction by the housekeeper, she would be assigned to care for the rooms of the young princes, who were undergoing strict military training at the time under the supervision of the major.

The next morning she was to present herself at the major's office, and she never forgot that interview. He shook hands with her as she entered the office, saying, "Sister Sitenhof, I am a Christian, and I know you are also. I am your friend." *So this,* thought Yente, *is God's messenger to me, like an angel in disguise.*

He seemed to know every detail about her, even to the date of her conversion. They prayed together before he explained to her the duties she would be expected to perform. The dignity and importance of this man's position were evident to her. His quiet, calm, and yet authoritative way of speaking was mingled with kindness and understanding. He was about 60 years of age, white-haired, broad-shouldered, and had a military bearing. He cut an impressive figure.

"My child," he said, "if you are ever in difficulty, come to me, and I will try to help you. Do not let the servants engage you in conversation, and apart from courtesy, do not mingle with them. There will be opposition," he said. "Some may be against you, but do not let it worry you. I will stand behind you." With these reassuring words he dismissed her, and, as if in a dream, Yente commenced her duties.

The housekeeper, a large heavyset woman with a Prussian background, frowned openly when she met Yente, first because she looked too frail and inexperienced, and second because she suspected she was a "foreigner." But because the major, who was the respected head of the household, had recommended her so highly, she was silent. Yente learned well and applied herself to her duties, and before the week was over, the housekeeper knew she was a reliable worker. Above all, the unobtrusive way in which she went about her work, without taking time out with the others to gossip, broke down all opposition to her appointment. The housekeeper found no fault with her.

What a relief it was for Yente to have a regular and dignified position like this, enabling her to discontinue some of the tortuous jobs she had been doing for more than two years. She did continue selling her country produce early each morning, which enabled her to feed her children butter, eggs, and apples. With her new work in the royal household she was able to eke out a little more than a mere existence.

On weekends she took the children on their weekly picnic in Brusselsberg, a suburban beauty spot where they could sit under large trees. They ate their own food at a picnic table, and Yente ordered, without embarrassment, five glasses of hot chocolate for the children and coffee with whipped cream for herself. All week she and the children looked forward to the picnic, and when they reached the top of the hill she became like one of them, playing their games, romping in the grass, hiding behind trees, and feeding the squirrels.

At such times she looked so young and carefree that other picnickers thought she was the nursemaid until, to their astonishment, they heard the children call her Mama.

Yente's faith in the Lord grew stronger day by day. At the end of a perfect picnic day, when the sun was setting, she loved to assemble her children around her, and, before returning home, they lifted their hearts to God and sang hymns they knew so well. Sometimes strangers gathered around the little group and joined in. When the folks who came there to picnic discovered that Yente's husband was a missionary in South America, their interest grew. They wanted to know more about this unusual family whose joy in the Lord, from the oldest girl down to the baby, shone in their faces.

Old Soldiers Never Die

On the third floor of their house an old pensioner, *der alte Herr Riehm,* lived in a garret room. His maiden sister kept house for him. He was 81 and looked like the typical Santa Claus of picture postcards with his long, flowing, white beard, twinkling, deep-set, blue eyes, and sparkling sense of humor. He was a veteran of the Franco-German War of 1870. The children loved him, a love reciprocated with mischievous affection. They teased each other mercilessly, but the day always ended with the children gathered around the fire at old Papa Riehm's feet, listening to his exciting and inexhaustible war experiences, which he drew from an unfailing memory and a lively imagination.

He smoked a yard-long, curly pipe, and the children loved to watch his venerable, wrinkled face through the smoke. Often Yente was able to do a little extra work at night and leave the children happy in the care of Mr. Riehm. He had no one in the world besides his sister, and so he claimed and enjoyed as his own the five little soldiers who looked up at him as the hero who had won the Franco-German War almost single-handedly.

He remembered each child's birthday with a little gift. He would tie the gift on the end of a string and dangle it out his window until the birthday child threw open the window below and claimed it by pulling it in, amid the laughter and excitement of the others.

But Mr. Riehm was an unbeliever, and Yente pleaded with him over and over to put his trust in Jesus. At first he scoffed good naturedly and paid little attention to what she said. But when he realized the strength of her faith and the important part it played in her life, he became interested. One evening toward the end of 1913 Yente stopped him on his way out for his evening stroll and asked him to make a decision for Christ there and then, to ask the Lord to forgive his sins and prepare him for eternal life. "Before it is too late," Yente told him, "accept Christ as your Savior, and you will experience the peace that passes all understanding." He broke down and accepted the Lord. "If He means that much to you," he said, "then I will give Him a chance to mean that much to me. Your life has been a testimony to me of what God can do for a child of His. I too accept Him as my Savior."

With those words the old man left the house. That very night on his way back to his upper room, he missed his footing and fell backward down two flights of stairs. Papa Riehm died instantly. Yente's family was grief stricken, but in her heart there was a song, for she knew that the old man died a believer and that his Captain was waiting to welcome the old warrior home.

11

The Powder Keg

IN THE SPRING OF 1914 tension in Europe was mounting daily. Long dormant national antagonisms, which had been smoldering across the continent for more than 50 years, accumulated enough explosive passions to blow up and bring about a holocaust such as the world had not seen to that day.

Germany was feeling her oats after defeating France in 1870 and imposing a humiliating peace upon that republic. Her industries were growing, but markets were dominated chiefly by powerful "John Bull" ruling the waves. France was still smarting from the humiliation and defeat inflicted upon her by Prussia and was waiting for the day when she could settle ancient accounts with her eastern neighbor. And in the East, the empire of the despotic czars felt called to unite, under the shield of "Little Mother Russia," all the Slavic nations of Europe.

Then there was the Austro-Hungarian Empire under Franz Joseph II, made up of a vast conglomeration of Slavic and Balkan nations built around the backbone and strong arm of the German and Hungarian national element. It was a hodgepodge of nationalities seething, striving, wrestling for independence, jealous and suspicious of each other, smarting under ancient wrongs—a veritable powder keg.

The match to light this powder keg was the assassination, on June 28, of Archduke Ferdinand, Crown Prince to the throne of the Hapsburgs of Austria. He was murdered by a fanatical student while visiting the city of Sarajevo in the little kingdom of Serbia, cocky because of its alliance with Russia.

The Beating of the Drums

In Germany, more than elsewhere, there was the certainty of impending war. People were not asking whether, but how soon war would come.

The public places and show windows of elegant stores in Kassel were decorated with colored reproductions of Kaiser Wilhelm II, resplendent in his uniform as field marshal of the army and wearing on his head the sharply pointed, tall helmet of a German military commander. His steely eyes, upward-pointed and well-waxed mustache, and chest covered with decorations and shining medals bespoke confidence and defiance.

The Kaiser's picture was accompanied by those of the stern and imposing field marshals and generals, Von Moltke, Von Ludendorf, Von Hindenburg, and others.

The passing public looked admiringly and with pride at them. Even when their lips were silent, their eyes seemed to say, *Surely with these great men leading us we cannot possibly lose.*

The strains of *Deutschland, Deutschland, Ueber Alles* came from beer halls, patriotic meetings, and military bands leading marching men. Through the streets of the old garrison city of Kassel one could hear the steady tramp, tramp, tramp of hobnailed boots as soldiers marched with the precision of a well-oiled and well-drilled machine.

The atmosphere was charged with confident and belligerent patriotism. Foreigners and strangers were automatically suspect. What were they doing in the Fatherland? Surely they must be spies.

Suspected, Unwanted

Yente could feel the people looking at her and her family. Even at work some of her fellow servants looked askance at her and asked among themselves, "What is this Russian Jewess doing here? Is she a spy too? Why doesn't she pack up her family and go to Russia where they belong?" Yente continued her daily work as conscientiously as ever, still able to muster a smile. Although she appeared calm on the surface, there was turmoil in her heart.

What will I do, she wondered, *if war should come?* She was alone in an enemy country with five young children. Where could she go?

Benjamin's last letter from Buenos Aires, dated May 25, 1914, was rather vague about his return, although he did mention that he might take a boat to Europe sometime during the summer. But on July 20, upon her return home, a telegram from England was waiting for her. Benjamin had arrived in London sick and could not continue his journey. A letter was on the way.

A fierce midsummer storm with thunder and lightning was gathering over her head. Would she be caught in the hurricane, unsheltered and unprotected? Would she and her loved ones be swept away like helpless leaves torn from a tree? "Oh God," she prayed fervently and feverishly, "show me a way out, open a door of escape."

Go!

On her way to work she ran into her good friend, the major, who greeted her warmly. He could see in her face that Yente was deeply disturbed. Her usual smiling eyes were now filled with unrestrained tears.

He was a friend, of that she was certain. He would do everything to help her. The major invited her to his office to discuss her position. He advised her that she must leave the country immediately, even if it meant separation from her children for a time.

Yente's mind was in a whirl. What was this disaster that had come upon her so suddenly? Was this what she had slaved for all these years, hovering like a mother hen over her nest, trying to protect her chicks from harm and hurt? Was she now to be separated from her children, without knowing when they would be together again? Must she leave the little ones in a hostile country at the mercy of strangers?

Yes, the major did mention Christian friends. But who would take care of five children? They would each have to be placed in a different home. Her poor children! How could she do it? What a decision to have to make.

That day Yente went about her chores in a mechanical way, her mind hardly knowing what her hands were doing. Yet an intelligence greater than hers guided her hands at their accustomed duties.

In the evening, after feeding the children and putting them to bed, she fell to her knees and poured out her heart before her Lord, asking Him to lift the burden so suddenly thrust upon her. She asked Him to undertake for her and the children and, whatever His will might be, to make it clear to her. She got up from her knees strengthened.

And then the doorbell rang. She opened the door, and there was Sister Paula, a Christian nurse whom she had known among the people at the chapel. She had come to say good-bye to Yente and her little friends. She whispered in confidence that she had received her mobilization papers from the army and was to leave the next morning. *So that's it,* thought Yente. *War is sure to come at any moment.* Sister Paula begged her not to mention her mobilization papers to anyone since it was still a secret. But she wanted to warn Yente. And she was anxious to say good-bye to the whole family, especially her favorite, Lydia. She walked into the bedroom where the child was sleeping peacefully, stroked her dark, curly hair, and crept downstairs on tiptoe.

Within the next three months, Sister Paula gave her life as a nurse on the front lines in East Prussia.

Benjamin's Return to London

At last Benjamin's letter arrived. He was laid up in a room in London, he wrote, with a high temperature and a racking cough. The doctor had warned him not to move. Kind friends from a London missionary society were attending to his needs, but traveling in his condition was out of the question.

He was conscious of the danger to Yente and the children in Germany if war should break out, and he begged her to come to England, without the children if necessary, so that they could work together from the outside to get the children out of Germany. "Leave everything," he said in his letter, "and come quickly."

When she finished reading the letter, Yente thought, *How strange that Benjamin and the major, unaware of each other, should have the same plan for me. This must be the Lord's will.* In spite of the heartache and uncertainly it would bring, she had to go through with the plan. Oh, how could she be torn from her young children, especially Lydia, barely six years old?

Of course Herr Sommer offered to have his godchild, Marie, stay in his home. He wished he could take all the children, but Mrs. Sommer and he were now advanced in years and would not be able to do justice to all of them. He telephoned several Christian friends, inviting them to come to his home and discuss the situation.

At the major's advice, Yente did not continue her chores at the princess' household. He told her to wind up her affairs within the next few days, and the time of her departure should be as soon as her exit permit came through. Yente got busy.

The three large wicker hampers stored in the basement were brought up, and all her worldly possessions, accumulated through years of wanderings, were packed in them. The precious down and featherbeds given to her by her father-in-law, Abraham Sitenhof of blessed memory, before she left Warsaw some years ago were placed at the very bottom. They could absorb a lot of shock. The little bits of china and crockery were packed in between, along with a few of the more precious possessions a family acquires as it journeys along life's winding path—*Rachel's domestic gods*—items that she found it difficult to abandon forever. Poor, pitiful Yente, pack yourself up again and go! But where?

The last time she had packed to travel from Warsaw to Germany, when she wanted to bring Benjamin back from Jesus to the faith of his fathers, she at least knew exactly where she was going. This time, not even that knowledge was granted to her. Where would she unpack her meager belongings? Where would her home be?

In the evening she went back to Mr. Sommer's home. The friends had gathered, and several expressed willingness to take the children to their homes. Fine old Mrs. Lembke, the dentist's mother, would be glad to have Elizabeth. She was already a big girl of 13 years and could certainly make herself useful after school. Her son the dentist would take Ernest. He lived in the suburbs and had a boy the same age, and the two could be company for each other.

Mrs. Berg, the wife of Henry, whom she had led to Christ, offered to take Jacob if no one else would have him. She had five little ones of her own living in cramped quarters, but if nothing more suitable could be found, he would be welcome. What her children had, he would have also. "Whether you have seven or eight mouths to feed does not make much difference, so don't cry Yente," she argued, scolding her lovingly.

But what about little Lydia? Oh, if she could only take Lydia with her. But no, that was not to be. The major had warned her to leave all the children behind. Otherwise the arrangements might be imperiled.

War

The assassination of Crown Prince Ferdinand of Austria triggered a chain reaction of explosions all over Europe. Exactly one month after that fateful event, Austria declared war on Serbia; Russia, the ally of Serbia, declared war on Austria; by August 1 Germany, allied with Austria, declared war on Russia; and England and France, allied with Russia, declared themselves on the side of the czars.

Ernest, a serious youngster with sad eyes, was 11 years old. Anxious to help his mother, he decided to become a newsboy.

On the first day of his new job, he came home with a few unsold newspapers bearing the screaming headlines, "Germany at War!"

Yente received the news calmly. Inside she knew that her faith was about to be tested to the utmost.

Little Lydia

Yente was now ready for the dreaded separation and journey. The only detail that remained was finding a home for Lydia. Yente had made an effort to find her a home with Christian friends but had not been successful. They were afraid that such a young child might be so attached to her mother that she would become homesick.

Lydia could sense her mother's uneasiness. She kept looking into Yente's beautiful eyes as if she were some unearthly creature or angel. How she loved to be with her—just to feel her presence. Conversation was hardly necessary. Her soulful, dreamy eyes did all the talking.

Lydia loved to take off her mother's shoes and bring her old slippers to her in the evening. That was her service and tribute to the mother she loved so dearly. If only she could give her mommy something that would express her great love. She was a little girl in love and felt love's almost painful necessity to give its all, its very life, its most precious gifts. But what could she, a little girl, give? She decided that one day, when she grew up, she would buy mommy the most beautiful slippers in all the world, red ones as soft and caressing as her love.

Finally a long-awaited message arrived from the Reverend Friedrich Wolfgang Lembke, pastor of a Lutheran church 80 miles away. He was the brother of the dentist who had agreed to take Ernest. In his letter the pastor said that since he and his wife had no children of their own, they would be glad to take care of Lydia. He would come the next day to take her home with him.

Now everything was settled. The children were all being cared for, and Yente was free to leave on her journey the next day.

That evening her friends in Kassel gathered around her, all wanting to do something for Yente and the children. Mr. and Mrs. Berg brought a hot meal for the family, so that Yente would not have to do any cooking in the midst of packing. Prediger and Mrs. Sommer came to say good-bye and to speak to the friends who had promised to take care of the children.

After a season of prayer with her friends, they all bid Yente good-bye and Godspeed. Some embraced her fondly and wished her a speedy reunion with all her loved ones. Then they departed. Yente was left alone with her children and with her God.

She put the children to bed with exceptional affection and tenderness. None of them knew as yet that she was going to leave. Why should she rob her darlings of one night's sleep before her departure? The morning would bring sorrow and heartache enough. Only Elizabeth had been taken into full confidence. Yente looked with longing and infinite sadness at each child, reposed in sleep and blissful innocence.

She stayed up the rest of the night, thinking and praying. The Lord was her Shepherd and the Shepherd of her little ones. Surely He would guide them to green pastures and still waters.

The last bit of packing was completed. Tomorrow Yente would pick up her papers at the major's house and go straight to the railroad station. It would be August 12, Lydia's sixth birthday. She felt a strong urge to cry—but no, she must not give way to weakness. Later, on the train perhaps, she could let out her pent-up emotions, but now she had to be strong.

12

Rachel Weeping
for Her Children

T HE NEXT MORNING there was a hushed silence at the
breakfast table. Yente recalled in her mind the day three
years ago when Benjamin had departed for South America.
There was the same tugging at the heart, the same feeling
of sorrow and yearning for dear ones still with you, and yet
already missed.

The children, all dressed in their Sunday best, questioned
Yente about where they were going. They knew they were
leaving the house, but how could she tell them the truth?
If she told them the arrangements she had made for them
and that they would be scattered like leaves shaken from a
tree by strong winds, she would break down. She would be
in no condition to travel. She would have to abandon all her
carefully arranged plans. It was too much for her. It would
be more than the children could bear. One by one she put
them off, seemingly hard and cold, saying, "You will find out
soon enough."

After breakfast, Mr. Sommer's sister, known to the family
as Aunt Bess, came to escort them all to the station. Lydia
stood in the corner, as was her habit, thumb in mouth, her
big, sad eyes looking with bewilderment on the hustle and
bustle of the last moments.

What was going on here? Dread seized her heart and squeezed until it hurt. She clung to her mother, eyes ablaze with unspoken and unanswered questions.

At last they were ready to go to the station. Each child carried a little bundle of belongings, Lydia dragging along the beloved doll mommy had made for her from some small scraps of material. Each one was spic-and-span with shoes highly polished. The girls' dresses were starched beautifully, their hair brushed and combed. Their short pigtails looked as if they too were starched. Each face was a study of bewildered emotions—youthful eagerness and anticipation of the unknown mingled with fear and anxious foreboding.

The farewell was quick, the children scarcely realizing what was happening.

Yente had told Elizabeth and Aunt Bess to take Lydia away as quickly as possible. They crossed the big square to the station, Aunt Bess telling the children that mother was going to get the tickets. In a flash Yente was gone, without as much as a kiss.

Lydia looked back with a bewildered expression on her face. As if from nowhere, Pastor Lembke and his wife joined them. He immediately diverted her attention to the small doll she was holding, commenting on what a fine doll it was. Lydia grasped it eagerly as if for comfort. "Come with me, little girl," he encouraged her. "I have many beautiful dolls in my home, and you may play with them."

One by one the children left the little group. Elizabeth was taking her brother Jack to the small village outside Kassel where he would be staying with a relative of Mr. Sommer's. Ernest was asked to follow Mr. Schneider. Quickly they entered a waiting cab and drove away. Aunt Bess embraced Marie and hurried away.

A Child's World Breaks Like a Bubble

Lydia felt that strange things were taking place in her small world. Somehow everything seemed to be melting away before her eyes, and her mind was in a turmoil of confusion. They again crossed the station square that led back to the city, but her eyes did not leave the spot from which her mother had disappeared. She felt someone holding her hand, but she dared not turn her head to look, fearing she might lose sight of that spot. And then, in a rush, reality broke upon her like the angry billows of a stormy sea.

A man and a woman, each holding one of her hands, were taking her away quickly, away from her darling mother, away from life and its very essence. She was blinded by hot tears streaming down her face. Who were these strangers? She had never seen them before.

Marching as to War

In the meantime, Yente entered the railway carriage, and a flood of grief and heartache finally overwhelmed her. She broke down completely and sobbed until the train left the station. There was nothing she could do but leave her children in the hands of God and pray for a speedy reunion.

With the clairvoyance and intuition given to those filled with great love, which sometimes borders on the supernatural, she could see clearly the terrible experiences waiting for her *orphans* at the mercy of strangers in an alien land—at war.

The train was filled with soldiers going to the front. The cars were decorated with national flags and boastful inscriptions: "To Paris!" or "Victoriously we shall defeat France!" At every station wives and children, sweethearts and friends gathered to see their men off. They waved flags and broke out in patriotic songs. "The Watch on the Rhine," "Germany, Germany Above All," and military marches that had become so familiar during the last few weeks were sung heartily to the accompaniment of local brass bands.

In spite of everything going on around her, Yente felt completely alone. She sat in the corner of her compartment glancing at the jubilation that greeted the train at each station as new soldiers boarded after saying farewell to relatives and friends. There was much laughing, along with the suppressed crying of mothers, wives, and sweethearts. It seemed that they would never stop coming, these soldiers with their knapsacks and families. More cars were added to the train as it continued on its way, all the while gathering more soldiers and military equipment.

As they traveled westward, they passed trains going in the opposite direction toward the east. These trains, however, were marked with different inscriptions such as, "Express to Moscow!" or "Russia is done for!" They too were filled with soldiers, some young recruits with the fuzz of youth on their chins, and some bearded reservists, all dressed in the gray uniform of the Imperial and Royal German Infantry.

Yente wondered how long the journey would take. It normally lasted two days, but in war time there was no telling. It might even take a week or more to reach neutral Holland.

The major had given her an envelope that morning, but she had not as yet opened it. Now she took it out of her pocket and unsealed it. Inside she found her ticket to England via neutral Holland and extra money in Dutch and English currency. How thoughtful of him. He had indeed proved a worthy friend.

By nightfall Yente was so exhausted that she sank back into her corner and tried to sleep. But the din of the military bands, now apparently traveling on the train, made sleep impossible. She was in such an exhausted state from the mental and physical strain that she could not relax.

On arriving at the German-Dutch frontier, the train stopped for inspection. War breeds fear and suspicion. Every stranger was a potential enemy or even a spy. Consequently, custom and passport inspection dragged on for hours. Yente wondered if she would ever reach London. The passport official looked at her with suspicion. When she produced her papers, he asked numerous questions and shook his head in bewilderment. What was this beautiful young woman with a tear-stained face doing on a military train?

Finally, after more than two weeks of travel and being shunted to sidelines to allow the passage of trains with wounded soldiers, her train reached Hook of Holland on the English Channel. There she embarked on a small cross-channel boat for Harwich.

At night she sat on the deck, saturated with the fine spray of the sea and her own tears and shivering with cold. All night long she swayed with every motion of the boat, torn with grief. The words of Jeremiah came to her memory, words she had read only a few days before:

> Thus saith the LORD, A voice was heard in Ramah, lamentation, and bitter weeping; Rachel, weeping for her children, refused to be comforted for her children, because they were not. Thus saith the LORD, Restrain thy voice from weeping, and thine eyes from tears; for thy work shall be rewarded, saith the LORD, and they shall come again from the land of the enemy. And there is hope in thine end, saith the LORD, that thy children shall come again to their own border (Jer. 31:15-17).

"Oh, Mother Rachel," cried Yente, "I know your grief, for I too am a mother, and my children are not. Oh, that the God who comforted you might also comfort my aching heart."

It seemed as if the gray mist of time between her and her distant ancestress, Mother Rachel, had suddenly disappeared. She was weeping for her children; her mother Rachel, the wife of Jakob, the Russian soldier, had been trampled to death by the hoofs of the Cossack horses giving her life for her little ones; and that other Rachel, the matriarch of the Hebrew race—all had become one. It was a kinship of flesh and blood that was very real and keenly felt. But it was more than that. It was the kinship of suffering womanhood, a kinship of all mothers through the ages who, since the days of Mother Eve, have cried over their beloved Abels and wept for the crimes of their ungodly but no less beloved Cains.

At dawn the English shore near Harwich appeared on the near horizon, and the sight stirred her mind with memories of her first visit to England some 15 years ago. When she disembarked in Harwich, there was the same suspicious scrutiny of the custom and immigration officials as on the German-Dutch border. Her Russian passport was in her favor, for the empire of the czars was the ally of England. But this woman coming from Germany, already at war with England, was a puzzle just the same.

Finally, after checking and rechecking her credentials, she was admitted to England and boarded the long train that would take her to Liverpool Street Station in London. On the way, hungry and weary, she ordered breakfast, a poached egg on toast, marmalade, and a large pot of strong tea. She felt better now and was confidently looking forward to a reunion with her husband.

In London Again

When Yente arrived at Liverpool Street Station, Benjamin was not there. Instead, two ladies, who introduced themselves as Miss Taylor and Miss Fried, greeted her cordially. They embraced her warmly and explained that Benjamin was at home with a slight fever. He had wanted to come to the station, but the mission doctor absolutely forbade him to do so. Again her heart felt heavy. A horse-drawn hansom cab took them through the East End of London, where Benjamin was waiting for her in a small upstairs apartment.

Looking at the wan face of her beloved husband, she was torn between joy and concern. Three years is like an eternity when separated from a loved one—and he looked so thin and pale. She would quickly mother him and coax him back to health.

They talked for hours, each full of questions and tales of experiences that filled the years of absence from one another. But overshadowing the joy of the reunion was the constant remembrance that their children were alone among strangers in Germany. They must find a way to bring them to England as soon as possible. They would leave no stone unturned. They would storm Heaven and earth to bring this about.

13

The Enchanted Village

THE TRAIN JOURNEY from Kassel to Roedeldorf where Rev. Lembke was pastor seemed like a nightmare to six-year-old Lydia. She sat in deep silence, stunned and numbed from head to toe. At any moment she expected to wake up and hear the comforting voice of her dear mother. But mother was far away.

When they finally reached their destination and her escorts hustled her off the train, Lydia came to the realization that she had been lured away to a strange place. Then she began to fight for her freedom. In the train they had said very little to her; but now, on the dusty country road, they tried to explain that they were taking her to their home to live with them for a while.

For the tired little girl, this was too much to comprehend. Like an outraged and trapped animal, she fought, weeping, kicking, and even biting the hands that led her.

The Lembkes had no children of their own and did not seem to understand Lydia's emotions. In vain they tried to calm her. They did not realize that to the youngster it seemed that they had walked and partly dragged her along past mountains and farmsteads, over bridges and through wooded sections—a tedious journey—to the village of Roedeldorf. Actually, the entire trip was only two miles from the railroad station, but measured by the imagination of a tired and bewildered child, it seemed like a long journey into captivity.

The village was like one pictured in fairy tales. In spite of herself, Lydia stopped weeping and took in the quaintness of the hamlet. The baaing of sheep as they crossed a narrow bridge greeted her ears. A sheep dog and shepherd boy followed close at their heels. In the distance a tall church steeple towered over the horizon. Just then the bells started pealing out their sweet music. What was that? It sounded so familiar. Yes, it was an evening hymn that her mother used to sing, "Take Thou my hand and lead me."

Hot tears filled her eyes. Mrs. Lembke, sensing the pathos of the moment, took the child's hand and drew her to herself. At heart she was a kindly woman, but she was intimidated by her overbearing husband. It was the first gesture of understanding and sympathy Lydia had experienced since that morning.

By the time they arrived in Roedeldorf, the sun was sinking in the west. Worn out by the emotional strain, the little girl submitted to the woman at her side and walked quietly the rest of the way, always coming closer to the church in the village. In spite of her grief, she could not help feeling that she was walking in a fairyland. At a glance she took in the many delightful details of the scene. Her first impressions of the quaint hamlet of Roedeldorf remained with her always, a memory of beauty and sadness.

The main street of the village was narrow and cobbled. On either side were storybook-style white cottages with steps leading up to the door. Then came the narrow bridge with two handrails over which a shepherd with a staff in his hand was crossing. Under the bridge ran a clear, cool stream from which came the croaking of frogs.

They passed a large sow and four little piglets, which made Lydia, who had never seen a real pig, cling to the lady. How white the baby pigs were; they looked so clean and scrubbed. Their little tails curled in an upward spiral.

Soon the church came into full view—a beautiful structure much like the picture in her storybook. Across the road from the church was the manse. They stopped and the man said, "Well, here we are at home."

The Manse

They entered a gray, austere-looking, stone, two-story house that was much too grand to be called home. Immediately a coldness gripped the child. A large English bulldog came bouncing down the stairs straight to his master, and, standing on his hind legs, it reached up to the man's shoulders. "This is Brutus," said Mrs. Lembke. "Don't be afraid of him because he loves children, and I know you are going to be friends." Lydia had never lived in a home with a dog. This magnificent animal, with his sleek brown coat and the big blue tongue of a pedigree, fascinated her. The maid, Lieschen, an apple-cheeked country girl whom Lydia learned to love, greeted them warmly and immediately took charge of her.

She was led to a second-floor bedroom that was to be her very own. A large imposing bed greeted her as she entered. The thought of sleeping all alone in such a big bed made her shudder. She was used to cuddling up to her big sister Elizabeth, and on occasions the three girls had shared a double bed. Something about the room chilled her.

"You can leave your door open, Liebchen," said Lieschen, "if you are not used to sleeping alone. My room is right above yours, and I will hear you if you call."

There was something reassuring about Lieschen as she took the child into her arms and pressed her to her ample bosom. Her sense of security, so suddenly and rudely shaken, returned for a moment.

Lydia took in some of the details of the large hall out of which all the bedrooms opened. There was a black ebony stand containing many long smoking pipes. On the front of the stand was a selection of leather dog whips, some plaited and quite thick. She wondered why one dog needed so many whips. But she soon forgot about it. Also in the hall were two large black cedar chests, and she wondered what was inside.

99

"That room," said Lieschen, pointing to a formidable black carved door, "is the study of the pastor. You must never enter it unless you are invited, dear child." Later the sight of that door would send chills down her spine.

Supper in the dining room was brief and sparse. Lydia was so wrapped up in her tearful thoughts that she hardly heard Pastor Lembke as he told her they wanted to be kind to her and be her friends. He explained that her mother had gone to England to meet her father, but because of the war between Germany and England it was not likely that she would see her mother in the near future.

After supper, as if looking for some diversion for the child, they took her upstairs, undressed her (not without a struggle), and gave her a bath. It would have been embarrassing enough if Mrs. Lembke had attended to her, but when the pastor himself proceeded to bathe her (saying how much he enjoyed children), Lydia was outraged. *Who are these horrible people,* she thought to herself, *and why do they persist in tormenting me instead of leaving me alone?* After the bath, slippers and a nightgown were provided, and the special treat the Pastor had promised her all evening materialized.

The Doll That Could Say "Mama"

They took her to the attic and showed her large boxes full of toys. There were dolls of all descriptions—baby dolls, dolls that could say "Mama," large dolls, small dolls, and medium-sized dolls. There were toys for boys also, but Lydia had no eyes for those. Only the doll that said "Mama" held her spellbound. "These toys," explained the pastor, "are for our Christmas party at the church. Every child will receive a gift then, and if you are a good little girl," he added, "you will get one too."

At that, she stopped crying and felt somewhat consoled. She thought if she only had a doll that said "Mama," she would not feel so forsaken. The very word *Mama* somehow was comforting. Finally they put her to bed after Pastor Lembke prayed with her. She never forgot that prayer—at least not the voice of the pastor who uttered it.

Lord and Master of the Manse

Pastor Lembke was a typical Prussian, a pastor by profession only. His heart had never been touched by the kindness of the gentle Savior, the Friend of little children. He was a hard man indeed. In his domain he was lord and master, and he made sure that everyone knew that fact. In the Lembke household, his word was law. If his wife ever differed with him, she dared not utter a contrary word but had to silently endure the long speeches he was prone to deliver when he tried to make a point.

Accustomed to the caressing love of her mother and the companionship of her brothers and sisters, Lydia soon learned to avoid him. Days went by when she saw him only at mealtime. Meals were served in the dark, heavily furnished dining room where a shadow of gloom always seemed to hover around the table. At each meal the pastor enlarged upon his good intentions in providing a home for the child. Mrs. Lembke, as if to make up for the hardness of her husband, always said a kind word to Lydia when she could. She told her how much she had wanted a child of her own, but the Lord had never given her that blessing.

The first days of adjustment were very hard for Lydia. She was soon to learn the bitter taste of life among strangers. Her last thoughts as she went to bed and her first thoughts upon awaking in the morning were always of her mother, her brothers, and her sisters. She wondered how long she would be parted from them; and then the tears, which she tried so hard to suppress, would flow again. Lieschen was her one consolation. She was so natural, so solid, so easy to talk to and sympathetic. No wonder she found herself more often in the kitchen with Lieschen than anywhere else.

Lieschen sometimes took her to the cow shed, and she enjoyed watching the milking. Country life and animals were unfamiliar to Lydia. Lieschen also took her to the market square to do the shopping once a week—an outing she always enjoyed.

The news of the strange child at the manse spread through the village like wildfire, and all the children were anxious to see her.

The Pastor Rehearses

Every day at breakfast the pastor had a new rule for Lydia. He expected these rules to be followed religiously by a six-year-old child whose bewildered mind and cowed spirit simply could not take in all he said. There was to be strict silence in the house on the day before the Lord's day when he prepared his two sermons. Nothing short of a fire could bring him out of his study on Saturdays.

For several days each week Herr Lembke reminded her of this rule. Then at about 10 o'clock on Saturday morning a sonorous and pretentious voice thundered out, in measured cadences, the platitudes that Lydia soon knew well. Her heart sank. This went on for hours at a time. Even Brutus, who always lay stretched out in the upstairs hall, would tire of that intoning pastoral voice, get up, shake himself, and stalk downstairs.

Gifts for the Pastor

Lydia loved to sit in the kitchen and watch the peasants come to the back door with heavy baskets on their backs containing various kinds of food, their own products. There were sausages of all kinds, homemade breads, cheeses, chickens, and other country produce, all gifts for the pastor. The sausages were hung in the pantry "to ripen," Lydia was told. They were graded in size and variety—row upon row. There were beef sausages and pork sausages, long ones, thin ones, short ones, fat ones, dry ones white with age, and fresh ones with a roseate hue. Their aroma hung heavy in the air around the pantry. Lydia wondered when the pastor and his wife could possibly eat all those sausages. There must be hundreds of them! And always the peasants came and added to the store.

Lieschen explained to the child, to whom such a store of food was very strange, that it was customary when an animal was slaughtered for the pastor to receive a share of the sausages as a gift, so there was always a big supply of them in the pantry.

Lieschen also told her of another custom that made the little girl's eyes shine. Herr Staub, the farmer who regularly slaughtered pigs, promised that when the next pig was killed he would make some sausages to measure for Lydia. "What does that mean?" she eagerly asked. Lieschen replied, "They will measure you from ear to ear and make the sausages that long." *How interesting,* she thought, and she immediately speculated, by measuring with her little fingers, how long that would be. "And will they be my very own?" she questioned eagerly. "May I send one to my sister Betty?" "Of course," came the prompt reply. So Lydia eagerly looked forward to the day when she would be "measured" for sausages.

There was so much that was new to her in country life that the first days passed quickly. There were many things to see, things she had never seen, heard of, or experienced in her life in the city.

Frogs at the Sunday Service

The first Sunday in Roedeldorf was most memorable. Everyone arose early in the morning and tiptoed around as if there were a sick person in the house. The pastor could be heard moving around in his room preaching a sermon aloud as he dressed. When he at last emerged, he was dressed in a suit even blacker than the one he wore on weekdays. That and the stiff high collar struck terror in the child's heart.

At the breakfast table a long Psalm was intoned before the meal began, which, on an empty stomach, was quite an ordeal. Then they ate in utter silence. Toward the end of the meal the pastor said, "Lydia, my child, I want you to sit very still through the service and set an example for the other young children who always wriggle around in their seats, as if they had frogs creeping up their legs."

Frogs creeping up their legs? thought Lydia. *How horrible!* The sentence echoed in her head from then on. Mrs. Lembke took her by the hand, and together they crossed the street to the church. The bells were pealing out their beautiful song. Lydia loved those bells. They had fascinated her from the very first time she heard them.

She had been introduced to the bell ringer the day before, a youth of about 17 named Johannes, and she was thrilled to meet the person who could make those bells play so beautifully. "Would it be possible," she had whispered to Johannes, "for me to come up into the tower and watch you ring the bells? I would stand very still," she added. Immediately the expression on the youth's face changed to concern. "Never ask me that again," he said. "You are too little to go up to the tower. It's dangerous." She was thinking of this conversation when she realized they had reached their pew in the church, and the pastor, looking more serious and austere· than ever, trooped out in his pastoral grown and regalia, followed by the choir boys in white. Accustomed to the simplicity of the Brethren, this ceremony was new to Lydia. There had been none of that in Kassel. It had all been plain and homelike.

And then the pastor started intoning all that he had rehearsed so meticulously the day before. Lydia's thoughts wandered off into a dreamland, a land of freedom and glorious independence. Suddenly she heard another voice. It was the pastor's voice, but whispering softly into her ear, as if from a distance—"as if they had frogs creeping up their legs." She sat up quickly and felt her legs and knees to reassure herself that no frogs had entered the church to torment her. She told herself she must sit still; the pastor had impressed it upon her. Yet the thought of the frogs kept returning, and she found herself fidgeting and moving from side to side. After a while she thought she could actually feel cold clammy frogs creeping up her legs, and with tear-filled eyes she struggled to keep still. *Why did the pastor have to tell me about frogs?* she wondered. She would have been able to sit still if he had not mentioned frogs. Frogs belonged in the brook, not in the church—and why was the service so long and drawn out?

Everything was so different in this church—so cold. The big building echoed with the pastor's voice. The ceiling was so high and the stone walls so cold. Lydia suddenly looked up to the ceiling. There, nestled above the rafters, she could make out the shape of the bells. How exciting! From then to the end of the service her eyes remained fixed on the domed ceiling.

After the service there was much curtsying to be done before many people. Mrs. Lembke had rehearsed the curtsy with her the day before and remarked how well she performed it. That pleased Lydia. When the last parishioners were gone, the church was locked, and the pastor and his family returned to the manse.

Lydia, I Want to See You in My Study

At the dinner table the pastor said in a stern voice, "Lydia, I want to see you in my study after dinner." That was the first of many study interviews that she would never forget. The pastor went to the study, and five minutes later Mrs. Lembke, with a sadness in her face that Lydia could not understand, told her to go up. She sensed tension in the air as she entered the room for the first time.

It was a book-lined room elegantly furnished in heavy black oak with a very large desk. The pastor began his speech immediately in a low, earnest voice. He reminded Lydia of what he had told her before church. She was to sit still, but, to his horror (and his voice grew progressively louder), she had behaved just like the other children. She fidgeted in her seat, and instead of keeping her eyes on him, she looked at the ceiling of the church, dreaming.

He would not tolerate such behavior, and he wanted her to know this. His voice was becoming increasingly violent until, in a crescendo, he banged his fist on the desk. He gripped the child by the shoulders and gave her a hard shake. Lydia was so shocked that she could not utter a sound. Her big brown eyes filled with tears. She loosed herself from his grasp and rushed out of the room. "The next time you misbehave, my child, you will get a spanking," Herr Lembke called after her. In a panic she raced upstairs to the attic and into the arms of Lieschen, who drew her into her room and tried to comfort her.

The child trembled in terror. She could not remember her dear mother ever being cross with her. She was frightened, terribly afraid of this man in black with the big voice.

Like a trapped animal, she looked around fearfully. When Lieschen coaxed her to lie on the bed and try to rest, she gladly consented, and Lieschen's big warm arms embracing her were a great comfort.

14

The Misguided Guardian

T HAT NIGHT LYDIA cried herself to sleep, her heart burdened and torn between fear and longing for the comforting presence of her mother. When she awoke the next morning, she discovered to her horror that she had had an accident during the night. She was too frightened to leave her room, and when Herr Lembke himself came up to get her, he discovered it.

Then the storm broke. He flung angry questions at her like a sergeant: one, two, three. "Will this ever happen again? If so, I will have to apply the whip. I will not tolerate an untrained child." His voice rose in staccato tones, and he snapped. "If this happens again, my child [he never forgot to say "my child"], I will have to use one of Brutus' whips on you." With that he left the dry-eyed, terror-stricken child alone.

For the rest of the day she was banished, left with her tangle of thoughts and bewildered emotions. Finally, at 5 p.m. the maid was permitted to bring her supper but nothing to drink.

The following day the pastor informed her that her mother would probably never return to claim her. Therefore, the best and kindest thing they could possibly do would be to adopt her legally, so that she could stay with them forever. But of course, he added, he would have to teach her "how to be a lady" and not to have any accidents. Little did Mr. Lembke know what a nervous reaction his harsh manner had on the child and that fear alone was the cause of this new trouble. The child was frightened even to fall asleep. She tried to hold her eyes open with her fingers. But sheer exhaustion finally overcame her, and sleep descended on her harassed little body.

Mrs. Lembke, although sorry for the child, apparently had no say in this or any other matter. She kept her peace and suffered in silence.

At the next invitation to the study, that formidable black room, the pastor used one of the bulldog whips to impress on the child the terrible crime she had committed. All her imploring that she could not help it, try as she might, was in vain. Bighearted Lieschen suffered with the child. All her senses were outraged by the harsh treatment and indignities the little girl had to suffer. She had grown to love her and tried whenever possible to shield her.

Pea Soup with Bacon

The episode with fatty soup was indelibly imprinted on Lydia's mind. She had never been able to tolerate any kind of fatty meat. She had a definite aversion to it, and Yente had never forced it on her. Therefore, when a dish of pea soup containing pieces of fat pork (a favorite dish in Germany) was placed before her, she gagged and could not eat it. As punishment, Lydia was sent to her room without supper. But when morning came, the same soup was heated and placed before her for breakfast. Again she tried but could not eat it. At lunch and supper the same soup appeared on the table. Try as she might, it just would not go down her throat—she gagged. By that time she was terribly hungry, yet she could not eat the thick fatty stuff, made more repulsive with every heating. She missed eight consecutive meals. But in the end the gnawing hunger was too much to bear. Two days later, when the same soup was set before her, she swallowed the concoction without even realizing what it was. Hunger is a cruel sensation and can play odd tricks on a person.

The child's nervousness increased with every punishment. She did not get used to the whippings with the dog leash. On the contrary, it seemed to hurt more each time.

The farmer who promised to measure her for a sausage eventually killed a pig and gave Lydia a fine smoked sausage, measuring her from ear to ear. When she triumphantly came home with her trophy, the pastor told her that since the war would, in all probability, last a long time, they would have to store up all the sausages. As a result, Lydia never did get to taste the special, custom-made sausage. All of this only served to confuse and frustrate the child. It made her timid and shy. She wanted to creep to her room and be alone.

Brutus Protests

Usually Brutus, the faithful beast with the uncanny instinct given to some dogs, could sense Lydia's loneliness and grief and followed her around or stayed with her in her room. It was as if he wanted to say, "I love you and will keep you company." She reciprocated the animal's love, and often she hugged the big, unsightly bulldog. Many a time Lieschen would find them both asleep on the rug in front of the bed.

When punishments were meted out and the child wept bitterly, calling for her mother, the pastor would say, "The more you call for your mother, the more I'll whip you. Your mother is not coming for you. She doesn't want you, and we will keep you here." This terrified Lydia so much that she wept for hours at a time, and then Brutus would lie on the threshold of her door and whine his protest against human cruelty.

All God's Children Ought to Have Shoes

Lydia had one pair of shoes, and they were wearing out rapidly. The pastor had promised her a new pair for Christmas, and that meant being measured at the village shoemaker. Lydia looked forward to having a new pair of shoes almost as much as seeing her sister Elizabeth, who was living with a family in Kassel. This too had been promised as a Christmas gift.

Lydia spent hours outside the shoemaker's little store, pressing her nose to the window pane, watching the shoemaker's deft fingers as they fashioned shoes—large shoes, medium-sized shoes, and, best of all, small children's shoes. All the large and medium-sized shoes were black like her own. But the small shoes fascinated her the most. They were just the kind that would fit her own little feet, and they were in different colors. Some were brown for winter and some were even white for summer. How she craved a pair of new shoes, even if they were just black.

And then one day she found the shoemaker fashioning a piece of red leather into the most darling pair of shoes she had ever seen. Big tears rolled down her cheeks as she hurried home to tell Lieschen what she had seen. Lieschen assured her that, come Christmas, Lydia was sure to get a pair of shoes, maybe not red because they were so expensive, but they were sure to be brown. How proud she would be to go to Kassel to see her sister Elizabeth and her brothers in her nice new brown shoes.

Joy and Disappointment

A few days before Christmas thick, heavy snow came down. The pastor hired a sled with two horses wearing tinkling bells around their strong, shiny necks. Lydia was happily surprised to be invited to go along for the ride. What an unexpected treat! She enjoyed it to the full. But there was a catch to the treat, a bitter price to pay for an hour of enjoyment. On their way home, the pastor told her that he and his wife would be spending Christmas in Kassel, but they could not take her along to see Elizabeth as they had promised. The sled ride was an effort to make it up to her.

When Lieschen saw how grieved and disappointed Lydia was, she offered to take her to her own home for the holiday. She lived in a neighboring village and had a big family of brothers and sisters, and they would spend a wonderful Christmas together. This being a very practical solution (for they would save food if the house were shut up for a few days), the pastor readily agreed.

But what about the shoes? "Oh there is no time for them now," said Herr Lembke. "They will have to wait until after Christmas." And so the child's dream of new shoes never materialized. By spring the soles of her shoes wore away almost completely.

Christmas in Lieschen's humble home was wonderful. Everybody welcomed her, and what lovely gifts they gave her— two handkerchiefs, one hair ribbon, and even a small purse with five cents in it. She treasured that purse for many years after. For the first time since she had been parted from her mother, she felt real happiness, and when she crept into the big bed that night with Lieschen, she snuggled up to her and fell asleep peacefully, all tension and fear gone.

Herr Lembke Becomes a Schoolmaster

The next three months dragged wearily by for Lydia. The pastor enrolled her in the village school where two young men taught the children. But no sooner did school start after Christmas than both teachers were called up for military service, and the village was left without a teacher. Pastor Lembke stepped in and taught in their place. For Lydia this meant an added strain. Now there was no escape from his overpowering and terrifying presence. At home and at school, the hard and harsh pastor overshadowed her life.

She could not understand why Herr Lembke was so different from good Pastor Sommer. *Maybe,* she thought, *these two preachers belong to different religions and serve two different Gods.* Pastor Lembke's God seemed to be severe and exacting, a stickler for order and formality. Even the prayers offered to Him had to be rhythmic, sonorous, and in big, high-sounding words.

Pastor Sommer's God was different—a friendly, kindly God to whom you could speak just as you would to your own father. This was the God with whom her mother was familiar. This was the God she prayed to when she was alone in the darkness and frightened. But why did they call their God by the same name, Jesus?

Day after dreary day and week after weary week dragged on. There was no news from mother. A fiery wall of war separated them. As for her brothers and sisters, they were scattered among strange people in Kassel and neighboring cities, and Lydia had no opportunity to see them.

15

Children Adrift

ELIZABETH WAS PLACED IN KASSEL with Pastor Lembke's brother, Johann Albert Lembke, a dentist, who lived with his mother and family in a spacious second-floor apartment that included the dental offices.

At 14, Elizabeth was serious beyond her age. Always mother's helper, she never had time to play or enjoy a normal childhood. Now in the dentist's home she was allotted a small bedroom near the kitchen and told her duties. She was to clean the dentist's office and wash the breakfast dishes every morning before leaving for school. After school she was to help with the other domestic chores. Usually her breakfast consisted of two slices of coarse rye bread and a scraping of margarine with a cup of substitute coffee.

In one respect she considered herself fortunate. Her brother Ernest attended the same school as she did, enabling them to see each other daily. This brought Elizabeth both comfort and distress because Ernest's position was even worse than her own. The Schneiders, with whom Ernest made his home, were poor working people, and, although kind to Ernest, they had little themselves. Hunger shone through his big eyes, and his gangling, emaciated body gave conclusive evidence of his plight. Often cold and hungry, he was hardly in a condition to concentrate on his school work. Elizabeth decided to share a piece of her bread with her brother, concealing it in the top of her stocking until recess time came. Then she would hand it to him surreptitiously on the playground.

Elizabeth grieved for her younger brothers and sisters, especially Lydia, who had always clung to her. Her youngest brother, Jacob, was billeted with people outside of Kassel, and she knew little about his welfare. That also worried her.

When evening came, Elizabeth served supper to the family in the dining room. Then she was given a scant meal in the kitchen, usually a little soup or stew and a slice of bread. After that she was sent off to her duties—scrubbing the floor, cleaning the windows, and polishing the household silver. Even in the cold weather she was expected to clean the windows with icy cold water, which caused her hands to chap and bleed.

But what really filled Elizabeth's cup with bitterness was Mr. Lembke's son Otto, who was 14 years of age. An only child, he was spoiled and took grim pleasure in mistreating Elizabeth. He called her "the unwanted Jewess." His misdirected patriotic instincts caused him to see in the unfortunate 14-year-old girl an enemy spy. These names spread around among the children, and life at school became unbearable.

Since her mother had left about five months ago, no one had heard from her. Was she safe? Had she joined father in England? These were tormenting questions. Elizabeth's eyes were often red and swollen.

Whenever she and Ernest could get together on the playground, they held serious conversations concerning their fate and that of their brother and sisters. They seldom heard from Jacob, and when he did write, his letters were full of woe and grief for his mother, sisters, and brother. Oh, the anguish of it all! The weeks and months rolled by. It was almost Christmas, and the chances of being reunited with mother were slim.

Vivacious and pretty little Marie, always the fortunate one of the family, was the only one in good hands. In Prediger Sommer's home, she was treated like their own child, the darling of the family. If anything, they spoiled her thoroughly. She was the only one who was well-fed, well-clothed, and happy.

An Overheard Conversation

One day toward Christmas Elizabeth, eating in the kitchen as usual, overheard a conversation in the dining room between the "old lady" (as everyone called old Mrs. Lembke, the dentist's mother) and a visitor. It centered around the Sitenhof children. Elizabeth was all ears. The man said, "How much longer can the authorities be put off? The food situation is getting worse and worse for the German people. How can the Germans be expected to waste food on these alien children, five foreign devourers? I will try to get an extension for them this time, but it will be difficult. Were it not for the major, the children would certainly not be allowed to stay one day longer."

The visitor went on. "Why hasn't the mother communicated with them through neutral channels, when she promised she would set Heaven and earth in motion on her arrival in England to get the children out of Germany?" On and on the conversation went. The contemptuous description of her precious brothers and sisters as "devourers" caused Elizabeth to shed hot tears of humiliation that blinded her eyes.

A Joyless Christmas

Christmas drew near. Elizabeth had held out high hopes for the holiday. When her mother left early in August, she was sure that by Christmas all the children would be reunited with their mother and father as one family. Now hope faded, and grief increased. Everybody, adults and children alike, seemed to become less friendly toward them and were sometimes downright hostile. War, short rations, loss of loved ones, and strained nerves made everyone irritable. What were these alien children doing in Germany anyway? Why didn't they go to Russia where they belonged?

More hard work was heaped upon Elizabeth. There was no time for her to do her homework, and consequently she got into trouble at school. Otto was becoming more abusive in speech and behavior, while his parents took no notice of it. Her cup of grief was full and running over. Then Elizabeth conceived the idea of running away.

In desperation she went to see Prediger Sommer to unburden her heart to him and Mrs. Sommer. Elizabeth wept bitterly as she told of the months of cruel treatment and inadequate food. The Sommers wept with the child. She also told of the snatches of conversation she had overheard about the Sitenhof children, and how the suspense of waiting for news from her mother was becoming unbearable. "Can you do anything, Mr. Sommer?" she implored. "Perhaps you could see the major about it."

"Dear Elizabeth," said Prediger Sommer, "there is not a day that I do not try to contact your mother, but it is impossible. We are at war with England, and contact is out of the question. I am in danger of being branded as a spy," he concluded. He had personally stood security for all five children to the German authorities. "Hold on, my dear child," he consoled. "Do not be discouraged. The Lord will open the way for you to be united again with your parents." He comforted her, prayed with her, and gave her some money with which to buy extra food when hungry.

"Hold on," he begged her repeatedly, "and in the meantime I will explore all channels to see if contact can be made."

Christmas for Elizabeth meant extra work and waiting on the family. Otto by now was a nightmare to her. Before getting into bed she sat in front of her window, watched the street lights, and dreamed about the time when the family would be together again. Where was her mother now? She prayed for her every morning and night and during the day while scrubbing the floors on her knees. She recalled the events of the last three years and the struggle her brave mother had waged to keep the children fed and clothed.

Yet not all her memories were unhappy ones. There were also sweet recollections that were comforting and soothing.

She remembered the picnics on the Brusselsberg in Kassel when the laughter and frolicking of the children made her mother so glad. Oh, for those big, delicious sandwiches they used to eat, stacks of them. They were made with butter or drippings and sometimes even a few slices of wurst, that flavorful sausage, in between. How good it had tasted. Suddenly she realized how hungry she was. That very day her ration had been cut again. At dinner she was given a small plate instead of a dinner plate, and she did not get as many potatoes as she had previously.

At Christmas Pastor Lembke and his wife arrived from Roedeldorf to join his brother's family, leaving Lydia with the maid. Elizabeth had hoped and longed to see her little sister. She swallowed the hot tears of disappointment and managed to ask for some news about Lydia. At once she sensed an unsympathetic attitude, which burdened her even more. She heard the pastor complain bitterly about how "untrained" the child was but that in time he hoped to "remedy" that. He sounded so cruel, so much like his brother the dentist and his nephew Otto.

The next day Herr Lembke told Elizabeth, "I am breaking the news gently to Lydia that she will have to get used to the fact of never seeing her mother again and that we will legally adopt her as soon as possible." *How can he say such wicked things?* she wondered.

All Is Not Well on the Western Front

January and February dragged on. The news from the western front did not look good for Germany. The initial advantage the Germans achieved by violating Belgium's neutrality at the start of the war, and which promised quick victory over France, gradually gave out. It became a war of attrition.

The battles on the Marne and at Ypres stalemated the German war machine. The heavy-booted German army could march no further. They had to dig in in the muddy trenches and numbing cold of winter across the fields of France and Flanders.

It chilled the soldiers' bones and dampened their spirits. How long would it last? What would be the outcome? The only hopeful sign, from the German viewpoint, was on the eastern front. There the poorly equipped and disastrously generaled Russian army was crumbling under the onslaught of the better disciplined and organized German forces of his Imperial and Royal Majesty, Wilhelm II.

But in the West, the storm was gathering against Germany. England, slow to make a start, was mobilizing her forces and rolling up her sleeves in earnest. France was galvanized into patriotic fervor with the cry, "They shall not pass." Even the exiled Albert, King of the Belgians, was encouraging his people to resist the brutal aggressor.

Short rations, hunger, and general weariness were beginning to tell on the German people.

The Lightning Rod

By a peculiar quirk of the human mind, the five Sitenhof children somehow became a lightning rod that carried off some of the pent-up hatreds, frustrations, and disappointments of a few Germans. They were five hostages of fate. Elizabeth, of course, felt it most keenly. The care of her younger brothers and sisters and the uncertainty about her mother weighed her down. Elizabeth's sad eyes sent a message to all who saw her concerning the grief and anguish of a 14-year-old cast in the role of a mother.

One day Prediger Sommer called on Dr. Lembke and told the dentist that the German government was anxious to deport all five children to Russia, "where they belonged," as they put it. Mr. Sommer urged the doctor and his wife, as Christians, to take a stand together with him and vigorously protest such an outrageous plan. Prediger Sommer reminded them that they had promised to keep the children until their mother could fetch them, and they owed it not only to her, but to God, to keep their word. But his plea received a cold reception. Then and there he realized that he could count only on his own efforts and that the Lembkes would not cooperate with him. On the contrary, they would be happy to be relieved of the responsibility of Elizabeth. "Of course," Dr. Lembke said, "if she were permitted to stay as our permanent maid, we would look upon it in a different light."

Secret Plans

Early in April came the long-expected message from the major requesting Mr. Sommer to see him at 6 p.m. that day. On arriving at the major's office, which was heavily guarded, Mr. Sommer was beckoned into an inner chamber. An air of secrecy pervaded the room, and in the twilight Mr. Sommer could sense the tension surrounding this noble man of God who had such a responsible position in the service of his country.

"Brother Sommer," he started, "I have explored every possibility of getting these children, who carry Russian identification papers, out of this country legally, but I regret to say everything has failed. It cannot be done. We are at war, and no civilians can leave the country, whoever they may be.

"But," he went on, the muscles of his strong face twitching in determination, "these children must be reunited with their mother, whatever the cost. I have devised a plan, which, if it works, and with the Lord's help it will, is the only way I can see to get them out of Germany. It is a risk, a great risk, but we are, as Christians, to shun risks in the service of the Lord. Soldiers are courageous in battle. This is a battle of the most paramount importance for the bravest woman I have ever met. I have prayed about this for the last four weeks, and although I cannot yet see the successful end, I know and am persuaded that this woman's faith will not go unrewarded. Somehow God's hand will guide, and this family will be reunited soon—very soon."

Prediger Sommer sat in absolute silence, deeply stirred by the pathos of the drama developing before his eyes. Before he could respond, the telephone rang. The major answered, and Mr. Sommer's eyes continued to be fixed on that manly face in which strength of character and goodness were chiseled by the Master Craftsman, the Christ whom he served. Mr. Sommer followed almost breathlessly the play of the facial muscles and the flicker of the major's eyes. What was he saying? Nothing audible, but Mr. Sommer knew instinctively that the person at the other end had called in connection with the very subject that had brought him to this office.

"No," the major answered rapidly, almost as if giving orders to a battalion of men on the front lines, clip and clear, "the five children are my responsibility. They will not be deported, but they will be escorted if they must go, and I will arrange the escort myself. It will be to a neutral European country— not to Siberia, via Norway and Sweden. I am responsible and will account for them to the highest authority. That telegram should never have been sent. Send another correcting it in a courteous way."

What could it mean? wondered Mr. Sommer, bewildered at the sudden shaping of events. The major turned to him. "Prediger Sommer, all is well. The Lord has answered our prayers. Get the children together. They leave Kassel on the morning of April 7. It is the deadline the German government has set. Do you know of a responsible woman who could act as escort?" Immediately Aunt Bess came to mind, and he told the major how interested she was in the welfare of the children. "Settled," said the major with an air of finality. "The children leave with Aunt Bess on April 7. You have three days in which to get them ready. I will arrange all details by then." They shook hands and parted.

Prediger Sommer walked as if on air with a song of praise in his heart for God's wondrous doings. "Thou . . . hast dried the sea, the waters of the great deep; who hath made the depths of the sea a way for the the ransomed to pass over" (Isa. 51:10). Somewhere from the subconscious storeroom of memory this passage floated to the surface of his soul.

Things began to move fast. Elizabeth cried uncontrollably upon hearing the good news. It was as if the dam holding back her grief and anxiety suddenly gave way to waves of relief and joy. The thought of seeing Lydia and Jacob, both of whom she had not seen for seven months, and the prospect of being reunited with her parents were almost too much for her. She was, however, kept in the dark as to details. No one told her what their destination was, but trusting as children are, and knowing the faith her dear mother had in Prediger Sommer, she knew everything would be all right. She smiled for the first time since her mother had left and sang while she scrubbed the floors. She did not have much to prepare for the journey, for she had only two dresses, one change of underwear, a worn jacket, and the pair of shoes she had worn every day for seven months. The "old lady," Mr. Lembke's mother, had had the shoes repaired once during that time as a birthday gift, but now they were very thin all over. But what did that matter? There was a rainbow in her sky, and at the end of the rainbow was the lovely face of her mother.

16

There Were Giants in Those Days

I N LONDON, in the heart of the Jewish area of Whitechapel, there stands a four-story house bearing the inscription, in Hebrew and English, "The Hebrew-Christian Testimony to Israel." Numerous Bible passages in English and Yiddish on the walls make it clear to the passerby that this is a Jewish mission.

The house itself looks weatherworn and old. From the street a flight of stone steps leads into a fairly large hall where, since 1893, Jewish people from many parts of Europe have gathered. To these people, this place has become a spiritual haven, a home in a strange land, indeed far more so than their own cheerless, overcrowded homes ever could be.

The Hebrew-Christian Testimony to Israel was founded by David Baron, who was born in Russian Poland in 1855. In time the unknown Jewish lad from an obscure town on the eastern crest of Poland became one of the most distinguished names in Christendom. Someone alluding to his name punned, "David Baron of the house of David, a prince." And so he was—slight of build yet a giant in spirit. He was a man of God-given wisdom, charm, and great Scriptural learning—a contemporary apostle to the Jews. Above all, David Baron was a man skilled in the art of prayer.

Born in an orthodox Jewish home in Poland, the intelligent boy was to become a great rabbi.

Weary of czarist oppression and anti-Semitism, young David, together with his brother-in-law, conceived the idea of emigrating to America. But when they got to Berlin, a pickpocket deprived him of the means to continue his journey, and he came to England instead. There in the city of Hull, for the first time in his life, through the reading of a New Testament given to him by a Jewish missionary, he came in contact with the Messiah Jesus. David felt impelled to follow this irresistible Jesus.

His father, hearing of his son's conversion, was heartbroken and addressed a pathetic letter to "My lost son, David."

Weep Not, Father

Eleven years later they met again—the man who, in the meantime, had become a flaming witness for the Messiah and the aged father now on the threshold of the grave. Their meeting took place on the border of Russia and Germany. They fell into each other's arms and wept. With his father was David's sister who, seeing the affection and devotion of her brother, said "Weep not, father. Surely there is something that we do not understand. He does not look as if he has no fear of God in his heart, and the fact that he has come from such a distance to see you proves that he still loves you, which he would not do if he were a *Meshumed* [an apostate]."

Father and son communed together in the things of God until the Sabbath drew near. Reluctantly the elder Baron had to return across the border into Russia in order not to break the sacredness of the Sabbath. With tears flowing down his cheeks he said, "My son, I see that you serve the one God, the God of our fathers. It will prolong my life to have seen you and to be assured of this."

David Baron had received his commission from his Master, "Go and tell My brethren," and he obeyed. Of all the great sons of Israel who ever witnessed for their Messiah, David was among the greatest. Like Paul, he traveled the length and breadth of Great Britain and Europe, and even to deserted and desolate Palestine, witnessing to his Jewish brethren, seeking to open for them a new understanding of God's plan in the light of Christ.

In this high calling, Mrs. Baron, a devoted English Christian, was heart and soul with her husband. In 1892 the Barons returned to England from Palestine after Mrs. Baron was stricken with an illness as a result of the unsanitary conditions prevailing in the Holy Land in those days. Up to that time David had been employed by an English missionary society, but he felt the need for a testimony of believing Jews to unbelieving Jews. Thus the Hebrew-Christian Testimony to Israel came into being, a movement born of prayer and anguish of soul.

One day Baron was praying before God for two thousand pounds (approximately $10,000), a large sum of money for those days. The money was needed to purchase a house in which to start the work of God in Whitechapel. One thousand pounds were on hand; the Lord would have to provide the rest. The money had to be available by the next Saturday, and it was Monday already.

On Thursday morning a letter arrived from Lord Blantyre, a devoted friend of Israel, with a check for two thousand pounds, saying that he was definitely instructed of the Lord to send this money to David Baron.

The Court of Heaven

Another incident in the life of David Baron was characteristic of him. A Dutch lady left ten thousand *gulden* in her will for Mr. Baron's work. But when the will was opened after her death, as so often happens, her relatives contested it. A Dutch lawyer, who was the executor of the estate, wrote to Mr. Baron saying he would be glad to undertake the defense of the legacy on his behalf. Mr. Baron's reply was, "We never have recourse to earthly courts. We shall appeal only to the heavenly court."

The strange outcome was that after two years of squabbling among themselves, the relatives decided to give the major part of the inheritance, amounting to more than double the original legacy, to Mr. Baron.

Charles Andrew Schoenberger and Immanuel Joseph Landsman

Closely associated with David Baron was Charles Andrew Schoenberger, a man of unusual spiritual and intellectual stature. He was born in Hungary in 1844. Early in his life Charles also came in contact with the New Testament in the home of a Christian friend who was ill at the time. This led him to Christ.

In time he became a close friend of Israel Saphir, father of the famous Jewish-Christian theologian, Dr. Adolph Saphir. Eventually Charles Schoenberger became the brother-in-law of Dr. Saphir.

To further his Christian education, he emigrated from Hungary to England where his unusual qualities of mind, heart, and, above all, great oratorical powers attracted wide attention. He was offered important pastorates in many churches. But his heart was with his people, the scattered and twice-destitute Jews, homeless in body and adrift spiritually.

David Baron and Charles Schoenberger were the founders of the Hebrew-Christian Testimony to Israel.

Another man of unusual stature in this venture of the Spirit was Immanuel Joseph Landsman, a Jewish Christian from Russia. He too was a princely man, an outstanding linguist who could speak fluent Russian, German, Swedish, English, and Yiddish, in addition to being a profound Hebrew scholar.

These three formed a triumvirate of spiritual pioneers dedicated to the task of bringing Israel to Christ and Christ to Israel. "There were giants in the earth in those days" (Gen. 6:4).

Home for the Weary

It was a foggy November day when Benjamin and Yente, led by a deep-seated hunger for fellowship and spiritual food, came to the Hebrew-Christian Testimony to Israel. When they entered the mission home, Yente could feel in her throat and nostrils the sting of the fog outside penetrating even in the heated hall.

She looked around and saw a group of Jews, obviously from Eastern Europe. By some small differences in dress or manner, she could distinguish Jews from Russia or Poland and others from Hungary, Germany, or Austria. They were all sitting around a long table, most of them listening intently to a man of striking appearance.

He was rather heavyset with gray wavy hair, a high-domed forehead, drooping mustache, pronounced nose, and big, sad Jewish eyes—eyes that reflected endless pathos and tragic understanding. But there was a dignity about the man that somehow emphasized his *other worldliness*. A spirit that was not of this world radiated from him. Yente soon learned that this was Charles Schoenberger.

The Prophet Ezekiel Versus Dr. Ezekiel

Mr. Schoenberger was reading and expounding something from the Book of Ezekiel and was drawing a parallel between the Prophet Ezekiel and someone, apparently a modern rabbi whom, for the sake of emphasis and contrast, he called *Dr. Ezekiel*—a deadly parallel.

"Ezekiel," Mr. Schoenberger said, "came with a message from God—his heart burdened, breaking for his people, his eyes dimmed with tears because of the waywardness of his people. He could not escape the ministry that God had committed to him. It burned within him. But Dr. Ezekiel, dressed in the fine robes of the modern rabbi, was a pleasing kind of fellow. He could speak about everything under the sun—politics, book reviews, the need for betterment among the Gentiles, and of being favorable to the less fortunate Jewish brethren.

"In the meantime, the more fortunate brethren who arrived in the synagogue in their chauffeur-driven cars listened politely. They congratulated the rabbi on his fine speech and said they would come again sometime, business permitting.

"Ezekiel felt a personal responsibility for the souls of his people. He would pay with his own life—yes, his very own soul—if he did not speak the Word of God to them. Dr. Ezekiel drowned his audience in a flood of platitudes.

"What is wrong with Israel?" he asked earnestly. "Israel is far from God because she has turned away from Jesus, her Messiah. Israel and Christ belong to one another. Christ and Israel are inseparable. There is no healing, no salvation, no hope until Israel and Christ are at last united."

Such was the tenor of Mr. Schoenberger's message. His earnestness, his obvious sincerity, the pathos of his address, which came from deep within his heart, held everyone in its grip. The discourse lasted for about an hour, then Mr. Schoenberger invited his listeners to ask questions. They sat like a transported audience. The master violinist had touched chords—unknown and unsuspected chords—in the hearts of his listeners. They seemed unwilling to break the spell.

Why Do Ducks Have No Shoes?

Nevertheless, here and there some were frivolous and scoffing. They could be recognized by the flicker of superior smiles on their faces. They knew everything. They had heard everything and cared for nothing. Yente, looking at the scoffers, grieved in her heart. She remembered the words from the Gospel of Matthew, "neither cast your pearls before swine" (Mt. 7:6). She was hurt and saddened.

"Any questions?" Mr. Schoenberger repeated.

One ragged-looking man piped up in a rather squeaky voice, speaking in Yiddish, "Preacher, I would like to ask a question."

"What is it?" inquired Mr. Schoenberger. "Why do ducks have no shoes?"

About a half dozen people giggled. However, most of the assembled people were shocked by this frivolity and gave the offending man a crushing look.

"Shame on you," someone cried out. "Here is a man of God pouring out his heart before us, speaking to us in the name of God, and all you can do is try to show how smart you are. Is it any wonder that our people perish in darkness and exile?" "That's true, that's true," a murmur went up.

Hurt to the quick and grieved in his spirit, a torrent of flaming words came from Mr. Schoenberger. *He is not just an orator,* thought Yente, *he is a prophet of God.* Every word was like the finely balanced thrust of the sword in the hand of a master swordsman. First he exhorted and excoriated, stern as John the Baptist; then he pled like a father with his wayward children. Listening to him Yente thought, *Yes, there is a prophet in Israel, even today.*

At the mission, Benjamin and Yente found the home for which they had longed. When Benjamin first returned to London after his sickness in South America, and was incapable of working, this mission came to his aid. They found friends at the mission who took a personal interest in their lives and problems.

Gradually Benjamin recovered his strength and began to work again. But the burning question that filled their days and nights was, When will we see our children again?

Also at the mission, Benjamin and Yente met Gladys Taylor, who took a particular interest in them. She did all she could to help in their efforts to contact the authorities and obtain entry permits for their children from Germany. But all efforts seemed hopeless.

Their English, especially Yente's, was as yet far from adequate. In the opinion of the immigration authorities, they were Russian refugees who wanted to bring their children, who were still in enemy territory, to England. How could they entertain such an idea?

One of the officers said, "Why didn't you bring your children with you? No mother leaves five children in an enemy country at such a time. We cannot help you. Go home and wait until the war is over." How could Yente explain, in her broken English, the complications and the unbelievable position of a Jewish refugee tossed by every tempest and circumstance?

A month of fruitless running here and there brought no results. With every vain effort, the strain mounted. At such times Miss Taylor proved to be a real friend. She stuck by Yente through thick and thin. She encouraged and comforted her and made necessary contacts for her. When Yente seemed to break down, she ministered to her physical needs, putting her back on her feet again.

Yente prayed without ceasing, "Lord, open the hearts of the right men and the right doors, so that I may have my children back with me." Nothing seemed to be able to break or daunt her. The three men of God in the mission, along with the other workers, encouraged her and gave her hope that with the Lord all things were possible.

Christmas, sad and dreary, came and passed. So did the month of January, spent in ceaseless but unavailing efforts.

Inspector Strong

As an alien, Yente had to report to the local police station. One day while there she met the head of the Alien Department, Police Inspector John Strong. Inspector Strong was a man who had come up through the ranks. For years he had patrolled the streets of the East End along Whitechapel Road, Commercial Road, Mile End, Petticoat Lane, and scores of narrow alleys and streets of Jewish London, a vast city in itself, teeming with bustling, brimming, almost overflowing life.

Inspector Strong was the darling of the Jewish people. Although he was a Scot himself, he could speak Yiddish like a Jew. His familiarity with the Old Testament and constant personal contact with the Jewish people, coupled with his deep love for the Lord, instilled in him a real affection for the Jews.

He was well aware of their weaknesses, peculiarities, and idiosyncrasies. Sometimes he would even poke gentle fun at them, but there were love and admiration behind it. He also knew their Jewish virtues, their deep devotion, and the purity of their family life.

Many times he was moved by their touching loyalty and deep gratitude shown in the country of their adoption, England, which had opened its doors to them when they were fleeing before terror and persecution. They could be embarrassingly grateful to people who were decent and did not take advantage of them. In the eyes of the Whitechapel Jews, Inspector Strong was a marvel. He was a high government official who could, if he wished, push them around, browbeat them, and demand bribes of them through subtle methods, which was a common practice in Eastern Europe. But he did none of that. On the contrary, whenever possible he tried to help. For many Jews, Inspector Strong was the first Christian they had met who was not a Christian in name only. They sensed that this man was something more than just a Gentile. Some of the pious Jews, thinking in terms of the Talmud, would say, "Inspector Strong is one of the righteous of the nations of the world." But folks paid him the highest tribute of which they were capable by saying, "Inspector Strong has a Jewish soul."

Mr. Strong was a big man with a gruff voice that often camouflaged tender feelings. Yet there was nothing soft or sentimental about him. When he saw something wrong being done, he could be very harsh and stern until the wrong was set right.

After many years of service with the police, he had been promoted to the position of inspector and became the head of the Alien Department. All aliens coming to the East End of London had to pass through his office. No man knew their affairs, their fears, and their hopes better than Inspector Strong. When he had an opportunity, and there were many, he was not ashamed to speak to his Jewish friends of the Lord Jesus whom he loved and served. He never failed to mention that Jesus was the Messiah of the Jews.

Yente was inevitably led to this man and unburdened her heavy heart. She spoke to him half in English and half in Yiddish. Inspector Strong reminded her again and again that she could speak Yiddish. She did so, but looking into his very Gentile face, she somehow could not bring herself to believe that he could really understand Yiddish. On she went, telling her pathetic story as best she could in her limited and inadequate English. But her tears, anguish of soul, and the pain written in every motion of her body had an eloquence and effectiveness beyond words.

The inspector did not make any promises; he only said that with God all things are possible. He suggested that they commit the matter to the Lord in prayer, and in the privacy of his office they knelt and asked God to open the way. Then he sent her home saying, "If I receive any encouraging news, I will let you know."

People scoffed at the Sitenhofs when they said they were trying to bring their five children over from Germany and that they hoped to go themselves and get them. The derisive laughter seemed to echo in their ears. People saw them as foreigners, speaking with a strange accent amid unbelievably tangled circumstances, and daring to expect the impossible. But these poor, despised aliens looked beyond all impossibilities and inexorable facts. They saw God and believed Him.

The Vicious Circle is Broken

The family was caught in a vicious circle. The Russian Consul would not renew Benjamin and Yente's traveling papers unless and until the British gave them an exit permit. The British authorities, for their part, would not consider giving them an exit permit unless the Russian Consul would extend their traveling papers. As for the entry permit to get the five children into England, Yente did not even dare think about that for the time being. Sufficient unto the day was the evil thereof. When the time came, the Lord would undertake.

At last, around the middle of February, word came from "their" inspector, as they called him now, asking Yente to appear in the Home Office. She went with Miss Taylor, anticipating that there would be some paperwork in English. And indeed there was—she was given a long application form to fill out, which Miss Taylor helped her complete. Yente's heart sang a song of praise, and her feet seemed to be stepping on air.

The next day another message came from Inspector Strong. This time Yente was to appear at the Consulate for the Netherlands to apply for a permit to the now neutral Holland, which bordered on Germany.

It was in the Dutch Consulate that she had been refused this very permit over and over again, but this time her heart was at ease. Her Lord was at work, and who could say no to Him?

When she arrived at the Consulate, the permit was ready and was given to her without delay. This traveling paper from the Dutch Consul took the place of the Russian passport, which had by now expired. With this permit in hand, she went back to the Russian Consulate, and they too endorsed the paper.

A few days later the message came from the Home Office that Yente had been granted an exit permit, and her children would be permitted to enter England. All obstacles were seemingly swept away. The children were to be reunited with their parents after all. There was only one problem that still had to be surmounted, the important matter of transportation. Few civilian boats were crossing the English Channel at the time. German submarines were lurking in the narrow waters of the Channel, and civilian traffic was almost at a standstill. But by early March 1915 passage was secured. Yente prepared to leave London for the Continent. She was to meet the children on the Dutch-German border. Benjamin, in the meantime, would remain in England and continue at his job so that the children would have a home and food when they were brought to London.

The evening before Yente departed, Benjamin wrote several letters, in the German language, to Christian friends addressed, "Dear brethren in the Lord." Yente was to deliver these letters to their friends upon her arrival in Germany. Little did they know how incriminating those letters would turn out to be during this time of war, wild suspicions, and monstrous fears.

'Til We Meet Again

A few hours before sailing time, a prayer meeting was held in the Mission. Baron, Schoenberger, and Landsman committed Yente and her husband to the Lord. In view of the danger of the undertaking by reason of the war and the lurking enemy, they implored the Lord to cover His children with His mighty arm.

On March 17, 1915, Yente took her leave and said good-bye to the many friends assembled in Liverpool Street Station. They sang "God be with you 'til we meet again" as the train pulled out slowly amid the confusion of voices and noises of soldiers and civilians bidding fond farewells to one another. "God be with you 'til we meet again" rang in Yente's ear as London melted away in the distance, soon swallowed up in the smoke and mist of a premature spring.

She sat down in the carriage filled with soldiers. She remembered so vividly her departure from Kassel only six months ago. That time she was surrounded by German soldiers, enemies of the ones who were now accompanying her. What a change. What a unique experience. If she were to tell her story, these men would be persuaded that in their midst was a fiendish spy. The truth was that she was a lonely, heartbroken mother led by the hand of God to a rendezvous with her precious children. Could anyone but God do such things? Would anyone believe her?

Passports Please

Shortly after leaving the station, two passport officers entered her carriage. They were surprised to see a woman in civilian clothes among so many soldiers. Immediately they requested that she come to a separate compartment where they fired many questions at her: "What are you doing on this train? How did you get here? What is your destination?" She answered quietly and confidently, but her poor English worked against her. How could she learn the language in six short months while her mind was so preoccupied with her children?

They could not understand her story. There were too many ramifications, too many involvements. At Harwich there would be an official interpreter, and she would be thoroughly examined. In the meantime, they left her alone. For the remainder of the journey she prayed that the interpreter would be a man of God who would not only interpret her words but what was in her heart and help to set things right.

17

A Rough Crossing

U PON HER ARRIVAL AT HARWICH, Yente was taken by an immigration officer to a private office and told she would have to establish her credentials thoroughly before being permitted to embark for Holland.

An interpreter carefully questioned her, scanned her traveling permit, and examined her photograph and those of her five children. He scrutinized Yente's permit to enter Holland and appeared satisfied. The examination, it seemed to Yente, was endless. She was anxious, fearing she might miss the boat, but the officer assured her the boat would not sail until midnight and that she had plenty of time.

Blinding Prejudice

As the interpreter was handing Yente's papers back to her, he asked, "With whom did you say you left your children in Germany?"

"With good Christian friends," she answered promptly.

The expression on the man's face changed rapidly. "Christian friends?" he queried. "What do you, a Jewess, mean by 'Christian friends'?"

This unexpected change in the man's attitude astonished Yente, and she suddenly realized that the official interpreter was a Jew. By now his annoyance was obvious. "How is it possible," he went on, "for a woman like you to have 'Christian friends'? Are you saying that these 'Christian friends' would be willing to keep your five children while a war is raging—to feed them, clothe them, and house them for you without compensation? Woman, you don't expect me to believe this story, do you?"

His manner was stern and sarcastic. He turned to the immigration officer and spoke rapidly in English. An animated conversation followed, which Yente could not understand, but the phrases "impossible story" and "suspicious person" seemed to be the key words of their exchange. Fear gripped her heart.

"Oh, Lord," she silently prayed, "give me the right words to convince these men of my innocence."

She was speaking. It seemed she could hear her own voice as if far away. "I am a Christian Jewess, and I believe in the Lord Jesus as my Messiah. When a Gentile accepts the Lord Jesus Christ as Savior, we are one in the faith and fused together by a bond of friendship which only a true Christian believer can understand.

"Believe me, sir," she continued, "I have no enemies in Germany—only friends." Yente said this innocently and without hesitation. But after she said it, her voice seemed to echo back to her: *No enemies in Germany . . . only friends. No enemies . . . friends . . . friends. Yente there is a war on. What have you said?*

She realized she should not have made such a statement. She felt the blood leave her body and her knees buckle under her, and then she fainted.

When she came to, she noticed that the clock on the wall showed 11:50 p.m., and a woman in uniform was leaning over her with a bottle of smelling salts. In ten minutes the boat would sail. She was panic-stricken and stood up shakily. Then the interpreter reappeared from the next room, and her heart sank within her.

"Mrs. Sitenhof," he said, "you will be permitted to embark, but the examination will continue on the boat, and I will come along as interpreter. If the examination proves, as I believe it will, that you are a suspicious person, a danger to England, you will be returned to England tomorrow and arrested."

He said this with such finality that Yente could say nothing. She followed him quickly, praying within her soul, "Dear Lord, take over from here. Let me be united again with my children. Let my testimony to this Jewish man bear fruit. Give me courage to face the examination, and may Thy will be done."

Yente felt relieved. The raging sea of fear and anxiety suddenly subsided. Her heart was calm. *If the Lord is on my side,* she thought, *who can be against me?*

Yente was committed to a stewardess on the boat who ushered her into a small cabin. There she was undressed to her last garment. Each garment was held up to the light and searched for any possible hidden messages. Yente realized she was being held on the suspicion of being a spy. *No doubt the prejudices of the Jewish interpreter are playing a considerable part in this,* she thought, but she was remarkably quiet. The Lord was with her, strengthening her. Even her long hair was let down, unplaited, and examined. Then she was told to get dressed again.

Finally she was led to a larger cabin where four Englishmen and the same interpreter were waiting for her. On the table in front of them Yente recognized her few belongings, along with all her documents and papers. She also recognized the letters Benjamin had given her in which he thanked "the dear brethren" for their loving care of the children. These were the letters she was to give to the person escorting the children to Holland. In a flash she realized how the interpreter would construe the meaning of the letters. The picture was getting darker every minute. The interpreter looked at her with unconcealed contempt.

"Woman," he said, "I do not believe your story. It will take more than this to convince me of your good intentions."

Then, starting from the time she was married, Yente explained her whole story. She told how her husband had been disowned by his wealthy father because he had accepted the Messiah Jesus, and how, after a great struggle, she too had been converted, and that there had been great suffering ever since. "But," she added, "it has been worth it—the persecution and struggle. I would go through it all over again, if the Lord so willed."

Her blue eyes, dim with tears, shone with a strange light that did not escape any of the men. The interpreter tapped his fingers nervously on the table while Yente was speaking, and when she finished, he turned on her. "You were a traitor to your faith. You are capable of being a traitor to the country that has given you shelter."

With that he turned to the other men, and they went into a conference together. Eventually the interpreter said to Yente, "These officers will each examine you separately, and they will then reach a conclusion."

The night dragged on endlessly. Each officer questioned her in turn through the interpreter. By the time it was the last officer's turn, it was 5 a.m. A grayish blue half-light was peering in through the cabin's porthole—a harbinger of dawn.

Yente was worn out and begged for a drink. Some water and then tea and toast were brought to her, which revived her somewhat. The last officer was yet to interview her. He seemed to be the chief immigration officer, for he had an insignia on his uniform that the others did not have.

A Brother to the Rescue

He came straight to where she was seated, and Yente noticed (or was it her imagination) a kindly look in his eyes.

"Mrs. Sitenhof," he said, taking her hand, "I want to have the honor of shaking the hand of a courageous woman who loves the same Lord I love. I am your Christian brother, and naturally I am the only one who understands and believes your predicament. Not only do I believe your story and will allow you to enter Holland, but I will pray for you as you strive to regain your children. I will do all in my power to make your reentry into this country easy."

To Yente's complete surprise, he said all this in broken German completely ignoring the interpreter. Joy welled up in her heart. She burst into tears and said aloud, "Lord, I thank Thee."

It was a dramatic moment, yet only the forerunner of many more to follow. The awful burden of proving that she was not a spy had been lifted from Yente completely. The Lord is wonderful and to be praised.

The grueling experience of five hours of questioning had left her limp, but when the chief officer finally gave her a letter to facilitate her reentry into England, she had a song in her heart.

The boat docked at the Hook of Holland at 6 a.m. Sea gulls were screeching from the boat masts and piers. Yente had had no sleep, and her eyes felt as if they were filled with sand, but there was no time to sleep. She gathered her few belongings and boarded the train for Rotterdam.

There she would have to seek the help of the Russian Consul, representing his Imperial Majesty Czar Nicholas II, to get the children out of Germany.

18

The Miracle of Rotterdam

I N THE SPRING OF 1915, amid the raging war and the booming of distant guns, neutral Holland was an oasis of comparative peace. Hedged between France, Belgium, Germany, and the seething North Sea, her position was delicate and unenviable. Nevertheless, for one reason or another, her neighbors respected her neutrality.

When Belgium was overrun with the Kaiser's armies causing thousands of casualties on both sides, Holland extended her hospital facilities to the severely wounded of France and Belgium. All trains and every available vehicle, from vendors' carts to the royal limousines, were pressed into service to transport the wounded and dying of the allied nations.

The German assault was swift, complete, and unexpected. Now the streets of quiescent Holland were disturbed by the distant echoes of war and the sight of the wounded who had been called upon to defend their country from the tyranny of the megalomaniac Kaiser.

It was springtime in Holland. In the streets of Rotterdam a lone woman was trudging from one consulate to another—weary, hungry, tired. But Yente couldn't rest while her heart was torn with anxiety for her children in Germany and anguished by the sight of the wounded, suffering, and distressed people all around her.

The Red Cross worked feverishly night and day. The Salvation Army headquarters, where Yente had sought refuge, was pressed into service. Every bed there, as well as those in hotels and many private homes, was requisitioned for the wounded.

Yente went from one lodging house to another, sleeping here a night and there a night. During the day she pled with the passport and consular authorities to assist her in getting her children out of Germany. They seemed to think she was unbalanced to make such an impossible request when everything was in a state of chaos and confusion.

Two weeks passed, and all her feverish efforts were in vain. She had been to Amsterdam and inquired at the Russian Consul, pleading with the staff to intervene. She sometimes felt as if she were being swept to the edge of an abyss that threatened to engulf her. The beginning of the third week found Yente back in Rotterdam with no money, no roof over her head, and no bed in which to sleep. Her eyes were swollen from weeping.

She sat in the park and prayed, "O Lord, if it be Thy will, let this bitter cup pass from me." There was no one to whom to turn. *Will there ever be an end to all this misery?* Yente wondered.

Her body was becoming weak from lack of food. She drank one cup of coffee each morning from the Salvation Army canteen, and on she went, driven by some unseen, relentless, superhuman force. For two nights she slept on a bench in the park. By now her senses were numb to the hunger and cold. Would anyone help her? "Lord," she cried, "help me or take me away."

The Guardian Angel

One morning as she was stumbling through Parklaan Street in Rotterdam (where most of the foreign consulates and the offices of the Dutch authorities were located), blinded with tears and weak-kneed from hunger and exhaustion, she suddenly became aware of footsteps behind her. She hurried on, faster and faster, afraid to turn around, yet knowing all the while that those footsteps were trying to catch up with her.

"Woman, stop, stop!" she heard a man's voice calling behind her. No, she must not stop, she must run.

"Why do you run, woman, why do you cry?" came the voice. "Let me speak to you, I want to help." Overcoming the fear that gripped her thumping heart, she slowed down and turned around to face the voice. It belonged to an important-looking man. Authority was written all over him. She thought he might be an official who wanted to arrest her. "Let me help you," he said again. "Nobody can help me except God," Yente answered.

With that she was ready to start running again. But the man replied, "God does not come down to earth in person. He sends His angels instead."

Yente realized that the man who had followed her must be a Christian—a real believer. And suddenly her fears were gone.

All her efforts in Holland had failed. She was no nearer to a reunion with her children than she had been on the day she first stepped on Dutch soil. This must be the man whom God had sent to help her.

She was out of breath and shaking from running, but now a sudden ray of sunshine entered her troubled being. With the words "He sends His angels instead" ringing in her ears and tears of gratitude streaming down her face, she submitted to the gentle voice of the stranger.

"Let us go somewhere where we can talk quietly, madam," he said. "The streets are so crowded, and you look tired." He wore neither a hat nor a coat, as if he had departed from somewhere suddenly, on an impulse. His dark suit reminded Yente of the many officials she had interviewed in vain during the last three weeks. He seemed to know all about her—that she had no home, no money, and was hungry. He led her to one of the best hotels in the city, and she followed him as if in a trance. As he entered the lobby, the hotel staff bowed to him in deference. *They must know him,* thought Yente. *Who can he be?* she wondered.

He talked to one of the hotel employees and, turning to Yente, said, "This woman will show you to a room where you can refresh yourself. In the meantime, I will order something to eat in the restaurant where we can meet and talk things over."

She was too weary to think. She was led to a luxurious room, a room such as she had never seen in her life. Upon entering she caught a glimpse of herself in the mirrored walls, and the image confronting her made her stop short. *Can that be me,* she thought, *that pale, wan, swollen-eyed reflection over there?* She looked haggard. Her protruding cheekbones and blue eyes sunken and lined with dark shadows told the story of sleeplessness and harassment.

She turned from the reflection of the ghastly shadow of herself to the pleasant task before her. What a luxury it was to be alone in a room and to feel the flow of unlimited warm water on her weary body. She felt sheer delight at the bubbly soap and the joy of being clean again. She had always loved cleanliness. She would never forget that soul-refreshing half hour. Her heart sang a hymn of praise, "Lord, you did send an angel, you did. I know it. Thank you for sending a friend."

She went down to the restaurant refreshed. Her Good Samaritan was already seated at a table in a quiet corner. "Please eat first," he said, "before you tell me your story. For days I have been sitting at my desk in front of the window watching you running bewildered here and there in the streets. I could not work. Each day I became more restless, and today when you passed my window, I felt constrained to follow you and learn what was troubling you."

He said all this in German. Yente could see that he was a refined, cultured gentlemen, soft-spoken and sympathetic. She listened as he continued. "Let me talk while you eat," he said. The crunchy rolls, fresh soft-boiled eggs, sweet-smelling butter, and a variety of cheeses, combined with the fragrant aroma of coffee, fairly intoxicated her. Only then did she realize how hungry she was as she remembered that she had not had a real meal for many days.

"I want you to trust me," he said. "Tell me what or who it is you are searching for so intently, and I will, with God's help, do all in my power to help you."

Yente had expected him to tell her who he was, but he did not. She told him her whole story. He listened without a single interruption, his eyes fastened intently upon her. She finished by saying, "And then, when all else had failed and the Lord had tried me almost beyond endurance, He sent you to me. This is my story."

He took out a pencil and paper and said, "Mrs. Sitenhof, please give me all of your personal data and your documents. Now I realize why I had no peace of mind at my desk. The Lord had a job for me to do. You stay at this hotel for a few days, make yourself comfortable, sleep, eat, and rest. I will pay for everything, so don't worry about the expense. I will contact you as soon as possible. Please trust me. I know that your traveling papers and documents are precious to you, but without them I can do nothing. Stay here and pray that the thing which is seemingly impossible shall be made possible, for the Lord is able."

Yente was dazed by what she heard. When she answered, her voice sounded far away. "May I ask who you are and for whom you work?"

"That is something I cannot tell you, Mrs. Sitenhof," he replied. "It would be unwise, but I will tell you that I am in a position to help you if any man can. Your situation is unique and dangerous. It must be handled wisely. Do not even try to learn who I am, but commit me to the Lord that He may direct my ways."

With that, he put her precious documents, including the traveling paper with the family photograph, into his pocket. He bade Yente farewell and assured her that he would communicate with her soon, perhaps in four or five days. And then he was gone. Her eyes followed him through the door, and then she was left with her thoughts and stirred emotions.

A hotel hostess interrupted her reverie. Bringing more hot coffee, fresh rolls, and cheese, she urged her to have a good meal and retire. She could not help crying, her tears mingling with the strong, flavorful coffee in her cup. Then she was shown to a room with a clean, soft bed, and an adjoining bathroom. She began to feel weak with emotion. Exhausted and hopeful, she fell asleep.

She slept for 18 hours. When at last she awoke, she was unaware of her surroundings or the immediate past. Where was she? What had happened? And then it all came back to her. No, it was not a dream. She was awake. She even pinched herself to make sure. She looked around carefully. What a haven of peace that room was. Everything spoke of comfort and ease. How little of those things had been her lot in the past. "The Lord is good to me," she kept telling herself. "Indeed 'His mercy endureth forever.' "

Exchange of Undiplomatic Notes

Two days passed. Then on the third day her friend, the guardian angel, came to the hotel. His voice quivering with emotion, he told Yente to make preparations, for in two days she would be reunited with her children.

Had she heard correctly? Suddenly the room seemed to heave and circle around her. Her Good Samaritan, realizing her condition, made her sit down while he told her of the events that had taken place since their last meeting. There was a sparkle in his eyes, and he sounded slightly amused as he related the story.

"First I telegraphed the German government in your name to allow the children to travel to the Dutch frontier. Promptly they telegraphed back, 'We are shipping the five gluttons to Russia via Norway and Sweden in the next few days, unless they are taken off our hands immediately.'

"Then, in my official capacity as government attorney, I wired back, 'Unless you escort the five Sitenhof children safe and sound to the Dutch border by Friday of this week, the Dutch government will hold the German government responsible for the welfare of these children. Mrs. Sitenhof is now under the protection of the Dutch people, and unless you take good care of her children, substantial reparations will be demanded at the end of the war.'

"Upon receipt of this telegram, they wired back that the children would be escorted to Sevenach near the frontier between Holland and Germany and that they would arrive by Friday."

Yente reeled. It was too much good news. Could it really be true? The *angel* who sat across the table from her was also visibly stirred—there were tears in his eyes. Together they praised Him who delivers in time of trouble.

Then her noble friend began to outline the details of the procedure. First she was to go to Sevenach by train. There the station master would call her name, and she would disembark. The station master would then take her to his home and accommodate her overnight. In the morning she would go by train, to which the station master would direct her, to the Dutch-German border where she would be met by a man who would call her by her name. She was to follow him, and in due course her children would arrive.

Everything, he assured her, was arranged to the last detail. She need have no fear. All her needs would be taken care of.

Yente tried to speak, but words seemed to fail her. She could only blurt out, "Please give me your name and address so that my husband can at least write and thank you for what you have done."

But he would not. He simply took her hand firmly, shook it, and said, "Sister Sitenhof, you do not have to thank me. I already have all the thanks I need. I can now go back to my desk in peace, knowing that the Lord has used this humble servant. I wish I could escort you myself and meet those five lovely children for whom you have shed oceans of tears and grieved so much. But I cannot. The Lord be with you."

With that he left the room and walked out of Yente's life as suddenly and dramatically as he had entered it.

On the table were three envelopes. One contained all of Yente's documents; the second, a letter addressed to the Christian station master at Sevenach; and the third, six rail tickets from Sevenach to Hook of Holland and six first-class boat tickets for the sea crossing to England. In addition, there was English money, ten pounds in cash—a small fortune of $50.00 to see the family home.

Such was the miracle Yente experienced in the city of Rotterdam and which she recalled over and over again until her dying day. It was her testimony to her Lord who never fails.

Her faith had been rewarded.

19

All My Children

THE FIVE CHILDREN with their escort, Aunt Bess, were scheduled to leave Kassel Station early Sunday morning. The respective "foster parents" brought them to the station. There was a feeling of secrecy in the air, as if spies were being smuggled over the border.

Pastor Friedrich Wolfgang Lembke, upon hearing that Lydia was actually leaving his home to meet her mother, was quite irritated. He still cherished the hope that he could persuade Lydia to consent to be adopted and stay with him.

"So," he said, the morning before the departure, "you are going to see your mother from England. I feel sorry for you. What a funny language she now speaks."

He then took an old English book from the shelf and started reading the English words as if they were German. The result was a ridiculous mumbo jumbo. "That is the kind of language your mother now speaks, and she will make you talk that way also. Do you still want to go there? If you had any sense, you would beg me, and I would let you stay in our home."

But the offer held no allure for Lydia, nor did his threat frighten her any longer. She did not fear anything if her mother were there. Reluctantly they took the little girl to the railroad station in Kassel the day before her departure from Germany.

Lydia's joy and excitement were boundless when she found herself once again in the loving arms of her big sister Elizabeth.

151

Seven months of separation had strengthened rather than weakened the bonds of sisterly love. Betty was such a comfort to her, and Lydia clung to her and followed her around every minute of the time, fearing they might be separated again. There was little said—their hearts were too full. It was wonderful just to be together again, to feel the nearness of one who loved her and filled and satisfied her aching heart.

That night when they were in bed, Betty whispered to her that tomorrow they would be on their way to meet Mama. It seemed a lifetime to Lydia since she had used that wonderful word, and now she repeated it with reverence, in a hushed tone, lest someone should hear and deny her the thrill of saying it. With the word *Mama* on her lips, she fell asleep.

There was no time for breakfast the next morning. Each carrying her little bundle, Elizabeth and Lydia hurried to the station accompanied by the pastor's brother, Herr Lembke, the dentist. All the way he grumbled about having to rise so early on a Sunday morning for a bunch of alien kids.

The "old lady," his mother, who had made Betty work so hard before and after school for the last seven months, said her good-byes the night before. Very ingratiatingly she shook her hand, all the while muttering how unfortunate it was to lose such a pleasant helper in the house and how hard and costly it would be to replace her.

"Remember," she said, "when you go to that enemy country, England, how good we were to you and how we shared our last crust with you, Elizabeth. I hope you will always be grateful to your German friends." Betty curtsied and quietly left the room; and Lydia, copying her, followed close on her heels.

The Children Reunited

Ernest was already at the station when Betty and Lydia arrived. He looked so thin and emaciated from lack of food that Lydia hardly knew him. She ran up and hugged him, and tears of joy flowed. A little way off stood Jacob, quiet and unmoved—a pathetic little boy of ten with a small bundle tied in a red cloth. When Lydia ran across to him, he dropped his bundle and almost shied away from her.

What is the matter with him? Betty wondered, and, going over, she put her arms around him protectively. "I am hungry," he said, his big eyes looking up into hers, "and I want to see mother." *Hunger* and *mother* were the two words that meant more to these children than anything else in the world.

At that moment the fifth child, Marie, arrived, looking happy, well-fed, and spoiled. Preacher Sommer and his wife had taken good care of her, and she looked like a little rich girl next to her hungry and unhappy sisters and brothers. She was nicely dressed, had lovely brown shoes on her feet, and a new satchel slung over her shoulders. The other four looked at her through envious eyes. Imagine, brown shoes, and practically new too! The other four looked so shabby in her presence. The uppers of their shoes were patched, the soles were worn out, and their toes were protruding through. They looked pathetic and forlorn in their cast-off clothing. Elizabeth was happy for Marie. At least one of them had had a home and real friends.

She went straight to Mr. Sommer, and with hands outstretched, thanked him as best she could for the loving care Marie had received in his home. Tears of gratitude welled up in her eyes. There was no time for more. Whispered good-byes were exchanged, and the children were hurried into the train.

To Lydia it seemed as if a journey to a fairyland had just begun. In the compartment Aunt Bess gathered the children together and explained how important it was for them not to hold conversations with fellow travelers and to be as unobtrusive as possible. This was to be a special journey, and they must not attract attention to themselves. They were not to tell anyone they were meeting their mother or where they were going.

The air of secrecy especially appealed to Ernest and Jacob. They had so much to tell one another and soon withdrew to a corner where they exchanged whispers for a long time. Aunt Bess carried a basket from which she produced also had weak coffee for the children (strong coffee would not be good for them) and diluted milk (it went much further). The unforgettable journey proceeded.

At the Dutch Frontier

By evening they had reached the town of Sevenach on the Dutch frontier. As they were pulling into the station, the train attendant called their last name and motioned them to follow him. On the platform there were several Dutch people waiting to receive them. This was the end of the journey for Aunt Bess. A train was waiting to take her back. Marie clung to her and cried, asking her not to leave. But, after being told she would see her mother the next day, Marie hugged her doll tighter and resigned herself to going with the others. Jacob looked less forlorn and even smiled as he shook her hand. Ernest seemed to be enjoying the importance of it all and kept repeating to Lydia, "Be quiet, mother is coming soon." This only made Lydia more excited.

The folks who met them were lovely people. They told the children that they were to be their guests for the night. The next morning their mother would arrive. Unfortunately, they had to separate for the night since none could accommodate all five children together. The boys went to one home, Marie to a second, and Elizabeth and Lydia to a third. They did not attempt to separate Lydia from her big sister again.

A horse-drawn buggy was waiting outside, and they bundled in. Soon the boys were dropped off on the way, Marie was left with one of the ladies, and Elizabeth and Lydia were taken by another very kind lady to her home.

What a beautiful, clean house this is, thought Elizabeth. Every corner of the kitchen sparkled. On the table hot soup, sandwiches, and tall glasses of rich milk appeared, and the girls ate with relish. Soon they were shown to the attic, and Elizabeth undressed Lydia and put her to bed. It was an unfinished attic—very large and airy. The corners and shadows under the eaves frightened Lydia a bit, but she finally fell asleep to dream of the next day when she would again see her mother who had left so abruptly seven months ago—perhaps seven years ago—or was it in some previous lifetime?

A Day of Great Joy

Breakfast the next morning in the bright Dutch kitchen was a delight. The girls had never seen such a selection of cheeses, let alone tasted them. The fresh homemade bread, sweet butter, and good rich milk tasted better to them than any meal they had had in Germany for the past seven months. Lydia hoped the meal would never end and that the lady would continue offering her more of everything. She could think of nothing else and wished her dear mother could enjoy some of this delicious food too. Elizabeth hurried her along, saying that mother might get there before they arrived, and that would never do.

With a hug and a kiss for each girl, the kind Dutch lady quickly wiped tears from her eyes and escorted them to a waiting buggy. Ernest and Jacob were already in the buggy. They, too, were eager to tell of the wonderful breakfast they had had, still smacking their lips at the thought of it. Today they were in high spirits. This was the day they had dreamed of for seven long months.

At the station Marie and her host were waiting for the others, and Marie beamed with pride as she showed them the gift of a stuffed toy dog that her host had given her. Marie was always receiving gifts. She was everyone's golden-haired darling.

Lydia looked enviously at the toy, but soon everything else was forgotten as they were led to a room to await the arrival of their mother. Those last 20 minutes were endless. The boys played a game counting out the seconds on the big station clock, and Marie and Lydia vied with each other as to what they would say when they first saw mother.

Lydia was sure of her words. She would ask mother why she had gone away for such a long time, then she would tell her how much she would like a satchel like the one Marie had. She would also tell her that she needed shoes badly. But then she thought that the shoes really could wait—perhaps Santa Claus would bring a pair at Christmas. If only she could have a satchel.

Elizabeth rose at last—concealing her excitement as much as a 14-year-old can, and taking Lydia by the hand she started walking quickly. Her heightened senses had detected the sound of an incoming train. From where they stood they were able to see a heavy frontier chain stretched across the platform. At that moment a train came into view. It slowed down, gave a lurch, and stopped.

Mother!

The next minute Elizabeth heard the station master call "Sitenhof," and before the others were aware of it, she saw a figure alight—a tall, slim, dignified figure she would know anywhere—her darling mother. Letting go of Lydia's hand, she leaped forward toward the figure, under the chain, with Lydia at her heels—into the arms of mother. The others followed quickly.

One by one Yente kissed her precious children, tears of joy streaming down her face. Even strangers watching the reunion wept. How could anyone help crying? This haggard looking mother and her eager children, half crazy with joy, were the symbol of a world in the throes of war, of unspeakable heartache, of separation and reunion.

It was almost too much for Yente. Her pale face with the deep shadows under her eyes stood out in the sea of faces surrounding her.

A train on the opposite platform was waiting to take them back into Holland to the boat. The sympathetic station master hurried them to the train.

The compartment that Yente and her five children were given was small but private, and as soon as the train started, the flood of words broke. It seemed as if all the pent-up emotions of seven months—all the fears, anxieties, disappointments, and frustrations—found an outlet. The children fought one another for the privilege of speaking to their mother. Each wanted to be the first to tell her all that had happened, while the others remained silent. But that was impossible. How could they keep quiet when their hearts were almost bursting with eagerness and joy?

Yente needed five pairs of ears, eyes, and hands to satisfy them all at the same time. They each clung to her; they each bombarded her with questions, without even waiting for an answer. They pleaded with one another for the chance to say something to mother. "Let me say just one word," they urged each other.

At last Yente brought them to order. Elizabeth was to talk first, Ernest next, then Jacob, Marie, and Lydia—in order of age. But it was no use. These children (at least four of them) had had no parental love for seven months, and now the eagerness to be heard overshadowed all else, and they were almost frantic to have their say.

Yente wept softly with joy. Out of the babble of voices she understood one thing clearly. Her children had suffered and hungered. She looked at their feet. How shabby their shoes were, except Marie's. *I will get them all new shoes,* she thought. *And I will cook for them and feed them.* She would soon banish the pallor of their cheeks and the shadows under their eyes, telltale signs of prolonged malnutrition. Yente studied the faces of her children with infinite keenness and tenderness.

Elizabeth looked wan and tired. There was a sad, depressed look in Ernest's face. Jacob was most emphatic about being hungry and did not cease to tell her that. The boys looked neglected and ill-clad. *But the main thing,* she thought, *is that they are with me and are mine again. God has given them back to me.* "Oh, Lord, how I thank You," Yente prayed. Then she told the children to bow their heads, and they prayed together. She poured out her heart in thanksgiving and praise to the Lord for the miracle that had given her children back to her.

A hushed silence fell over them all. One by one the children became calm. The Lord was present in their midst.

Sailing Homeward

Yente finally told them that they were on their way to England. Soon they would be crossing the North Sea—maybe tonight or early tomorrow. The prospect thrilled the boys, for the spirit of adventure had gripped them. She told them not to be loud in their conversations with each other after they got on the boat in Germany, for Germany was at war with Britain, and the quieter they were on the way across the Channel, the better it would be for them. But that was a tall order. The children could speak only German, and after being suppressed for so many months, they longed to let off steam.

At 10 p.m. they boarded a small Dutch passenger boat at Hook of Holland for the trip to Harwich, England.

20

Encounter with a Submarine

Y ENTE WAS AMAZED to discover that the boat tickets for England were first-class and that they had two adjoining cabins. Yente and the three girls occupied one cabin, and the boys were next door sharing a cabin with two men who made a great fuss over them and supplied them with big chocolate bars and other treats. To the boys, the ship was a dream come true, and they made great plans to explore every nook and cranny the next morning.

It was fun chasing each other down the narrow winding corridors, to be free to play with a brother, and to have that wonderful feeling that loved ones were nearby. Both Ernest and Jacob harbored the same thoughts. To be a family again was too wonderful for words, and every now and then they put their heads through the door of their mother's cabin, just to make sure she was there.

Soon it was time to go to bed. Each boy had the privilege of sleeping in an upper bunk, and they enjoyed climbing the ladder up into their beds. This was an unexpected treat. In the next cabin Lydia and Mary (as Marie now preferred to be called) enjoyed the thrill of sleeping in the upper berths. And when mother, who had the berth below Lydia, pushed the mattress above with her hand to amuse Lydia, the little girl cried with sheer delight and excitement. How could one little body stand all that happiness? It was only when Yente took her into her arms that Lydia finally fell asleep.

The City of God

For Yente this was a night of prayer and praise. *This is how the children of Israel must have felt when they reached the Promised Land,* she thought.

What a great God she had, and what a great Friend He was. She felt so unworthy. The impossible, the utterly preposterous had actually happened. Here she was at last, reunited with her five children, leaving one "enemy country" to enter another country of "the enemy." What enemy? Whose enemy? She had no enemy. God had wonderful people in Germany, England, and, she was certain, everywhere in the world. She also knew that other people—hard, relentless, heartless people—were everywhere as well. But Yente was at peace with everyone in the whole world, and above all, she was at peace with her Lord.

Although she was poor and penniless, God had provided all her needs. She was a homeless wanderer without a country or a city, but she was certain that her God would also provide a city, the one for which she was looking, a city of rest and refuge, a city of God where He and those who love Him dwell. All her life she had longed for such a city. The thought came to her suddenly that this city could be anywhere in the world, that the city of God is where God dwells.

With dreams of God and His beautiful city of peace filling her head, Yente fell asleep for a while. Little did she know the turmoil the next few hours would produce for her and her children.

The ship had not left the dock yet. They were to spend the hours of darkness in the Dutch harbor and leave in the early hours of the morning for the crossing to England.

All kinds of people were aboard the ship—Dutch, Red Cross officials, and mostly refugees escaping the jaws of war and death. Each passenger wore a strained look on his or her face it seemed to Yente to be a look of dread. The crossing at a time like this was, of course, dangerous. German submarines were lurking in the North Sea in formidable numbers and often mistook neutral ships for enemy vessels, sinking them without warning. All over the ship there were notices in Dutch, English, French, and German about lifeboat stations and the use of life jackets.

The boys were thrilled when they tried on the life belts and were told what to do in the event of an emergency.

Yente awoke with a start. She could not hear the engines throbbing, and looking at her watch she saw that it was 5 a.m. But soon the boat was started and began to rock, a sure sign that they were out of the harbor and in the North Sea.

And then Yente prayed, pleading for a safe passage for her little ones, herself, and all the other souls on board. The Lord was very close to her during the early hours of that morning, and she felt His presence keenly. She was calm and peaceful when she ended her prayer.

By 7:30 a.m. the boys were up and dressed, and the girls soon followed their brothers. When they discovered they were on the high seas, they shouted for joy and clapped their hands.

After Yente inspected them to see if they had washed their hands, faces, and ears and combed their hair, they all trooped to the dining room where breakfast was served—their first meal together for seven months. Ernest's eyes wandered, and he was aching to explore the boat. Yente told them they would go to the top deck, get deck chairs, and sit down, and she instructed them to stay well within earshot of her. She wanted to be able to see them all the time and keep them close together.

Already they were the talk of the boat. A woman with five children who could speak only German, aboard a Dutch liner, en route to England—it just didn't make sense.

The sun was up high now and by 9 a.m. everyone seemed to be busy. Yente sat on the deck with Elizabeth next to her, while Lydia and Mary played ball nearby. The scene was very peaceful. Thoughts of a raging war or submarines lurking in the briny depths around them were forgotten for the moment.

At 9:30 a.m. Jacob came to Yente and reported that Ernest was lost. They had been playing hide-and-seek together when Ernest disappeared and could not be found. Two sailors hurried up to Yente and confirmed Jacob's story. They had searched everywhere, but to no avail. The boy had disappeared.

Yente was told to stay with the other children while the search continued. By 9:45 the captain himself came to her and, with a worried expression, told her Ernest could not be found. Her heart almost stood still. Could it be possible that he had fallen overboard? But he was a good swimmer, and surely someone would have seen or heard something.

Enemy Submarine

Suddenly a siren sounded, shrill and loud. Whistles were blown and orders were shouted everywhere. Confusion reigned. Yente stood as if rooted to the spot. That could mean only one thing—an emergency! The captain was shouting through a megaphone from his bridge, giving clear, concise orders: "To your stations, all life jackets ready. Keep calm. No immediate danger. Be ready."

Submarines were near. At that moment a sailor came stumbling across the deck with Ernest close at his heels. "Where did you find him?" she asked. "Aft at the flag," he quickly replied.

There was no time for further explanation. Ernest joined his family and, with a rather shame-faced look that pleaded for forgiveness, busied himself with the life jackets that were being handed to all passengers.

This was a tense moment, probably the supreme test in Yente's life. She strained every nerve to remain cool, calm, and collected so that the children would not panic. She surveyed the situation in a glance. A German submarine had stopped the boat. Even now, while the siren and whistles were blowing, the boat was slowing, and a sailor on the bridge was preparing to signal with his flags.

The captain addressed the crew and passengers. "Women and children first." It seemed as if he looked in the direction of Yente and her five children, who stood lined up below him.

"This is a Dutch ship," he said, "a neutral ship, and by international law it cannot be sunk. But we must be prepared," he went on. All eyes scanned the water below while life jackets were adjusted. Lifeboats were already being loosed.

A woman nearby screamed. Someone else became hysterical. The siren and whistles continued their warning, and the five children looked to Yente, the bulwark of their strength. She stood tall and slim with poise and dignity, calm and fearless. Then she began to sing the chorus:

> Only trust Him, only trust Him, Only trust Him now; He
> will save you, He will save you, He will save you now.

The children joined in quietly, as if hypnotized. Now they too were calm, and, placing their hands in one another's, their life jackets on, they stood ready to face anything. Their mother was with them, and they had nothing to fear.

The Lord gave Yente superhuman strength at that critical moment. As they stood holding hands, eyes fixed on the turbulent waves below, the sirens and whistles stopped, and a hush fell over the ship. It seemed as if a magnet were drawing all eyes to one spot where, slowly and silently, a periscope appeared above the waves about 100 yards from the boat. At first it looked like a stick coming out of the sea; and, as it grew taller and taller and began to move, everyone recognized that it was the dreaded German submarine.

They held their collective breath when at last the deck of the vessel appeared above the surface of the waves. "A submarine," gasped Ernest, who had read about them and seen pictures of them. "And it is a German submarine, Mother," he shouted excitedly. "Look at the flag—black, white, and red."

There was more signaling from the bridge, and the captain shouted through a megaphone to the figure that had appeared on the deck of the submarine far below the ship. Fascinated by the sight, all eyes strained and focused in that one direction.

When the Dutch identity of the boat was established, they waited for further orders.

The orders came, sharp and clear: "You may proceed."

It was all over. As if in unison, everyone heaved a sigh of relief, some laughed loudly, some burst into tears, and still others continued to stand and stare dazzled at the scene that had just been enacted and in which they had taken part. Slowly the submarine submerged and was lost from sight. For a while they observed, awestricken, the wake of the disappearing vessel.

Yente gathered her children around her, hugged and kissed each one in turn, and told them to stay close to her as she helped them out of their life jackets. She finally sank into a deck chair, and the children did likewise. They were all stunned by the ordeal through which they had just lived.

The Arrival in London

The remainder of the Channel crossing was uneventful. A luncheon was served just before they arrived in Harwich, England, and a spirit of expectancy pervaded the air. Again Yente warned the children that they should not speak German loudly or call to one another. She instructed them to whisper if it were necessary to speak. Just to verbalize the language of the enemy was to be labeled as one of them. Yente knew that next to earning a living, teaching the children English would be her biggest problem.

In the immigration office she produced her papers and the letter of recommendation the kind Christian immigration official had given her on her journey out of the country. She had no difficulty whatsoever reentering England with her children.

Once settled in the train en route to London, Yente's thoughts flew to Benjamin. From the Liverpool Street Station they would take a taxi and would soon be home.

21

Death in the Skies

IT HAD BEEN THREE YEARS since Benjamin Sitenhof left his family for Buenos Aires, and the younger children could scarcely remember him, especially Lydia.

Thus, when Yente led the children up the narrow staircase of the house where Benjamin and she had been living in the East End of London and presented them to their father, Lydia shrank away as if from a stranger.

Through tired eyes Benjamin looked at his family. Since Yente's departure he had been sick and remained in his room praying for them day and night. Now the Lord had brought them together again.

In the dimly lit, overcrowded room he sat up in his bed and looked from one to another in silence. It was almost too much to comprehend. The miracle that had taken place overwhelmed him, and he burst into tears.

Seven forlorn souls were brought together again at last. Each sad face bore the stamp of suffering, anguish, and hunger. Mary, who had the least to weep about, since she had been well taken care of and had suffered nothing, wept the loudest. But all the past anguish and the agonizing wait that climaxed in this happy reunion were bound to have an emotional outlet. Tears provided a happy release.

There was only one double bed in the room. "Where will the children sleep?" Yente asked. Benjamin put her mind at rest. The attic had been prepared for them for the night. Gladys Taylor had found an apartment for them and had gathered together a few pieces of household furniture from kind donors and friends. *At least they have beds to sleep in. Nothing else matters,* Yente reflected.

Russia Square Building

In the East End of London there is a section called Cambridge Heath in Bethnal Green populated chiefly by dock workers, brewery hands, road workers, and other such laborers. The section, which has a radius of about two miles, gets *hotter* the closer you come to the heart of it. The dwellings are big tenement houses—dark, dreary, dismal four- or-five-story buildings—where crowds of grimy, unkempt children play, scream, or cry.

In 1915 these buildings were inhabited by many drunkards and their families. Anyone who could earn a living and did not spend it on alcohol could not tolerate the place very long and soon moved away, at least to the outskirts of the section.

In the heart of this rather dismal part of London stood Russia Square Building, and the Sitenhofs moved to an apartment on its ground floor. London was already preparing for German bombings. Sirens were being put into action to sound air raid alarms. The police had special constables engaged to stand by, keep order, and see that everyone took cover. There was talk of zeppelins coming over to blast London off the face of the earth.

With all of these activities going on, the Sitenhofs and their five children, who spoke only German, the language of the enemy, moved into their new *home.* The beds that had been donated were carefully disinfected by Yente, and every piece of furniture was washed. When she was finished, the apartment sparkled as it had probably never done since it had been built.

The curious neighbors did not speak a word to them. Yente, sensing the hostility of the mob to anything German, instructed the children not to speak at all until they learned some English.

The first night after they moved in, the raids began. At 6:30 p.m. Benjamin came home carrying on his back a collapsible organ which he had picked up at an old curiosity shop for six pence. By 7:30 he had assembled it and was playing a hymn. The children were already in bed—the three girls in one bed, the two boys in another. As Benjamin played, they sat up in bed with big questioning eyes, unable to understand how such a small instrument could play such a beautiful melody.

"Your father is so clever," mother told them, "he can do anything from building a house to repairing old instruments." They remembered that he had always had a violin. Now it all came back to them—how in Kassel, Germany, he played for them, and there was always a little fable connected with the tune.

As he finished playing, there was a sharp knock at the door. Yente opened it, and a large man with a special constable badge on his coat entered quickly and slammed the door shut behind him. He immediately explained in a somewhat excited voice that Inspector John Strong of the police station had sent him to warn them not to leave their flat at all that night, or any night after dark. They were to lock themselves in and remain quiet. An air raid warning was about to be sounded since a raid was expected at any time. Their position as aliens who spoke only the language of the enemy was very dangerous, to say the least.

With that he was gone. Dear Inspector Strong—what a friend he was. He knew that they had moved that day, since Benjamin had reported their change of address at the police station.

Benjamin and Yente had no inkling how dangerous their position was. Ten minutes later a blast and a wail of the sirens went off. The noise was frightening. The people from the upper stories were already pouring down the steps. They took shelter under the stairs or pressed against the walls.

They Are Germans

The mob filled the small hallways and staircases. They pushed and cursed at one another, shouting in loud voices. Then suddenly someone remembered the new tenants, and word went around as to who they were. Questions were asked: "Does anyone know anything about them? Who are they, anyway? Why don't they open their door and at least let the children take cover?" Then someone shouted, "They are Germans. They were seen buying bread at Schmidt's, the German baker, today. Aliens—that's what they are—and they have the best flat on the ground floor. Let's get them out. Let's break down the door." All of this was accompanied by cursing and swearing.

On the other side of the wall, every word was clearly heard by Benjamin who quickly translated to Yente.

What tragic irony, they thought. Years ago murderous Russian hatred of Jews drove them from their native Poland to Germany. In Germany, they suffered as despised Russians. Then, faced with insane animosity, they moved Heaven and earth to get out of Germany, undertaking a perilous journey to England in the midst of a raging war. They defied enemy submarines lurking at sea and death raining from the air. And now, at last in England, the land of freedom and hope, they were in danger of violence at the hands of an excited mob incensed against everything alien, regardless of race or religion.

At that time a wave of fear and hatred toward foreigners was sweeping the country. People with foreign names were eyed with suspicion and distrust, especially if the name happened to be German. Many Schmidts, Schneiders, and Zimmermans, long established in England, became respectable and nonsuspect Smiths, Taylors, and Carpenters. Among the so-called better classes, the hostility against aliens was more subtle and restrained. But in the *Russia Square Building* mentality, amid the uninformed and semiliterate who never moved outside the precincts of the dock area, to be a *furriner* was to be an enemy of England.

"We are in real danger if the police do not come at once," Benjamin said, when a crash shook the house. It was the first bomb to fall on London in the First World War.

Screams of terror came from without, a hushed silence from within. Seven praying hearts throbbed excitedly in anxious expectation. In the hall there was a terrifying commotion. Angry people banged with their fists at the door and screamed in drunken, excited tones, and the three youngest children, Jacob, Mary, and Lydia, clung to their parents.

Then another crash sent the mob running into the street, the most dangerous place to be. Soon the raid was over, and the all clear signal, prolonged and penetrating, was given.

Sister Sarah

After a few weeks in this intolerable environment amid hostile people, Inspector Strong realized—more than Benjamin and Yente themselves—that it was dangerous for them to continue living in the Russia Square Building. He assigned a special constable to report the temper of the other tenants to him, and the reports were not good.

One morning he visited the tenement himself and informed Yente that he had located her sister Sarah, who was now married and living in Walthamstow. Sarah was expecting Yente and the family to visit her and, if possible, to arrange to stay with her.

Since there were rumors of trouble brewing in the building, Yente immediately packed a few things in a bag, took the children, and left. Benjamin had already received a message from their ever-faithful friend, Inspector Strong, advising him where they were to go as soon as he finished work that day. A taxi was waiting to take them the 12 miles to the east suburb of London where Sarah resided. Yente, who by now was used to receiving and carrying out orders, obeyed without question.

Sarah was waiting on the doorstep of a small row home with eager anticipation. She had not seen her beloved sister for 14 years. She had married in the interim and had a seven-year-old daughter and an infant son. Dear Sarah! She could not do enough for her sister's children as she busied herself to make them comfortable.

Makeshift beds had been set up everywhere. Chairs were pulled together to sleep one child. Mattresses were put under the tables for the little ones to protect them in the event of an air raid. Bowls of fresh fruit stood around for the children to eat and be nourished.

Aunt Sarah and fresh fruit seemed inseparable. In the years to come Lydia always remembered her first impression of Aunt Sarah's home—a conglomeration of furniture rearranged to meet the emergency and bowls of fresh fruit. The larger the bananas and pears, the better Aunt Sarah liked it. "Eat little children," she gently coaxed. "Fruit will make you healthy and beautiful too." The children needed very little coaxing.

Benjamin arrived at supper time, and then they received the greatest surprise. Aunt Sarah had been fortunate enough to find a house to rent right around the corner, and, although the cost was comparatively high, she rented it for them. "High" to the Sitenhofs was 15 shillings a week out of the meager 50 shillings ($12.00) Benjamin was earning at the time.

Yente made it a rule never to live in a new dwelling without first disinfecting and scrubbing every room, nook, and cranny, and this she did the very next morning. She had a very high standard of cleanliness and took every opportunity to teach her children that a clean life goes with a godly life.

A Sword and Not Peace

After a full day of scrubbing, hanging curtains, and preparing for the furniture to arrive, Yente sat up late with Sarah and talked. During the conversation, Yente witnessed to her sister of the wonderful way the Lord, the Messiah of Israel, had protected her and her family and the deep peace she had found since she had believed on the Jewish Messiah as her Savior. This was a blow to Sarah, something she never expected to hear.

As soon as she could recover from the shock, she voiced a cry of bitter disappointment and anguish. "How could you become a Meshumed?" she cried. "What has come over you since we last saw each other 14 years ago? Is this what Benjamin brought with him from South America?" She sobbed and wept as if a very dear one had just passed away. "What terrible catastrophe has overtaken my beloved sister?" she asked, amid tears.

Yente tried to explain the wonderful change and peace that had come into their lives since their conversion and how much they depended on the Lord Jesus Christ, who had never let them down. They loved the Messiah, she told her, and would pray that Sarah too would accept Him in due course.

The close sisterly relationship suffered a deep blow, and Sarah never showed the same warmth and affection to Yente. She built up a wall of prejudice between them; and although she still loved her sister, she looked upon her as a traitor and never really forgave her for her "change of religion."

Death in the Sky

A few nights after the Sitenhofs moved into the little row house, the bombing of London began in earnest. The zeppelins were seen trying to cross the North Sea, and one, the Graf Zeppelin, got through. The night of the Graf Zeppelin will forever remain in the memory of those who witnessed it, for such gruesome sights leave an indelible impression on the mind.

The family had gone to bed when sirens sounded, and neighbors woke each other by knocking loudly on the front doors. Unaccustomed as everyone was to this new method of destructive warfare and the confusion it naturally created, the family scattered before they could get organized.

There was shouting, the dropping of bombs, and the *ack ack* of the clumsy and inefficient antiaircraft guns of the First World War. Benjamin translated the shouts of the crowds outside. "They've hit it—the zeppelin's on fire. She will come

down on the houses. Leave your homes—get into the street."
Suddenly a tremendous explosion rocked the very foundation
and sent the children running after their parents, who were
already at the front door to see what was happening. It
sounded horrible.

But listen. Now the crowd of hundreds that filled the streets
was shouting, "Hurrah, hurrah, hurrah!" Looking up into the
sky, a scene of horror met their startled eyes. There was the
pride of Germany, the Graf Zeppelin, crippled and on fire from
stem to stern. Lydia watched the ghastly sight dumbfounded
and in terror. Inside the zeppelin she could see the outlines
of the men still strapped to their seats, burning to death. The
sight of the burning, staggering airship paralyzed her. Above
the roar of the crowd screaming incessantly, "Hurrah, hurrah,
hurrah!" (the only word she understood), she quickly realized
that men were being burned to death while other human beings
were cheering the gruesome sight.

She was confused and bewildered. Violence had been done
to the soul of a six-year-old girl. The crowd was jostling her
here and there, and, frightened and upset, Lydia hurried back
to the welcome shelter of their home, where she sobbed her
heart out.

The crippled Graf Zeppelin staggered and lurched another
five or six miles across the countryside then crashed at
Billericay, Essex, burying the poor charred airmen up to their
waists in the earth.

Later they erected a monument for the men who perished.
But in Lydia's memory the burning zeppelin remained a symbol
of cruel inhumanity—a crowd cheering men burning to death
in the sky.

22

A Hebrew-Christian Home

I N THE SUMMER OF 1915 Benjamin was employed in a factory that, before the war, made pianos but now produced airplanes, particularly the wings made of plywood, four to each plane.

It was a skilled and specialized type of work, and Benjamin was up to the task. He drew up the blueprints, an exacting job that had to be correct to the smallest fraction of a millimeter. He went about his work quietly and unobtrusively, saying little but working much and well. Although Benjamin's heart was in the mission field and his desire was to preach the gospel to his Jewish kinsmen, now that he had been called upon by the government to make his contribution to the war effort, he did the work "as to the Lord" (Col. 3:23).

In the moderate climate of England his health improved considerably. The heat of South America had been more than he could tolerate, but being one of the first to pioneer in Argentina, the Lord had blessed his three years of ministry to the Jews in Buenos Aires.

Now with a war on, it was his duty to do his part for the country that had so generously received him and given refuge to his loved ones. It did not take long for his superiors to notice the difference between his performance and that of the other men. But Benjamin was a foreigner, a newly arrived alien.. They could not promote him officially to a responsible position entailing the supervision of many native-born Englishmen. The intricate work requiring superior skill was, therefore, given to Benjamin almost in secret. Designs of planes were, of course, top secrets. Benjamin did the work, but an English co-worker was given the credit.

By nature, Benjamin was a dreamer with a scholarly bent of mind. Above all he was a humble man, and his supreme desire in life was to preach the gospel and win souls to the Lord. This desire so consumed him that often his family took second place. He echoed Paul's words, "woe is unto me, if I preach not the gospel!" (1 Cor. 9:16). The seeming conflict between his duties for his Savior and responsibilities to his loved ones was one of the tragic aspects of his life, not uncommon among men of single devotion.

Weekend with the Sitenhofs

Sunday with the Sitenhofs usually began at 2 o'clock on Saturday afternoon, when they all went to the East End of London to the mission headed by that illustrious man of God, David Baron. Yente hustled and bustled around the house on Saturday morning getting everything ready for the afternoon and Sunday, the Lord's day. The whole family traveled by bus or tramway (trolley) to Whitechapel. There was a stir in the mission house when the seven Sitenhofs walked in and filled a whole row.

Sometimes they were the only visitors besides the workers of the mission. The two hours they spent listening to the Word of God expounded by such princely men as David Baron, Immanuel Landsman, and Charles Andrew Schoenberger were a never-to-be-forgotten experience for each of the children.

After the service, tea was served upstairs in the mission house. Genial Mr. Baron, relaxed after the meeting, usually presided, telling amusing and interesting stories out of his vast experience. There were slices of buttered bread, jam, jelly, scones, dainty little cakes, and lots of strong, hot tea with milk. This was a ritual that both the mission workers and the visitors enjoyed greatly—a time of real fellowship. While tea was served to the rest of the family, Benjamin often went outside and handed out tracts or took part in preaching at the open air meeting that followed the indoor session. It was livelier out of doors, for the mission was located in the heart of the Jewish section, and thousands of Jews passed by each Saturday afternoon. They were all dressed in their Sabbath finery, strolling aimlessly past with eyes roaming here and there, watching for anything unusual to take place in which they could perhaps take part.

The sidewalk outside the mission was unusually wide, providing room for many people to gather around the speaker At the edge of the sidewalk were the vendors' stalls, selling everything from peanuts to fur coats, and all the venders shouted, offering their wares for sale. In Whitechapel there was a medley of Jews from all over the world. Whitechapel on a Saturday afternoon was as interesting a scene as one could hope to see anywhere. On Saturday evening, by the time the seven Sitenhofs were bundled into an overcrowded tram on their journey home, the younger children were exhausted, if from nothing else but the sight of such a motley crowd of people. Lydia invariably fell asleep in Benjamin's or Yente's arms.

On Sunday morning they worshiped with the Plymouth Brethren, which became their church home. Here Elizabeth, Ernest, and Lydia were baptized when they accepted the Lord Jesus Christ as their personal Savior. The fellowship with the brethren was sweet.

The house in Walthamstow soon had to be abandoned for the same reason as the previous tenants had left it. It was overrun with black beetles, which swarmed everywhere when left alone in the house for a few hours on Saturday afternoon.

One evening on their return from the mission, Benjamin had no sooner turned his key in the lock than a humming sound greeted his ears. He quickly lit the gas jet in the hall, and as he walked across the dining room he heard a sound of crunching underfoot. He told the family to remain outside and quickly surveyed the situation. The floor and all the furniture were black with beetles. A homemade spray with disinfectant, which he always kept handy, was put into action, and the horrible pests scurried away. But it took hours to clean up the mess. There was no sleep that night for the Sitenhofs; it was, instead, a night of prayer. "Lord," Benjamin and Yente pleaded, "Thou knowest our need and our means. Give us a clean house tomorrow."

The very next day a letter came in the mail. A Christian friend had heard that a house in nearby Leytonstone might be available for rent. It was a much larger house than the one in which they were presently living, and the owner was a Christian. Benjamin wrote to the lady, who replied that she had a buyer for the house, but upon seeing his need she changed her mind, and rather than selling it, she rented it to the Sitenhofs. "Before they call, I will answer" (Isa. 65:24).

Leytonstone is a refined suburb of London at the edge of Epping Forest. It was here, in a quiet neighborhood on a clean street, that the Sitenhofs had their first real home. It was an old brownstone-style, three-story, eight-room house. During the next seven years the Sitenhofs found much happiness there.

Strenuous conditions make children mature much faster. At 14 years of age, Elizabeth was almost grown up. There was no going back to school for her; she willingly began to help her parents. She found work in a dressmaking establishment in the East End, which, during the war years, made uniforms for the army. The family was so enthusiastic that Elizabeth brought home work at night and taught all the others to do it. Even Lydia, eight years old, worked on the "bobbins" (officer's braid). It was fun working as a family. Yente worked well, and Mary and Lydia also did their best. Because it was a tedious job, the boys soon tired of it. But the girls continued helping Elizabeth and mother earn extra money for food. It was quite an undertaking to feed and clothe five growing children during the war years.

Chemical Experiments and Magic Tricks

Soon Ernest left school and found a job in the laboratory of a chemical factory at Stratford. He had an inclination for experimenting, and chemistry fascinated him. His special hobby was photography, and when Yente suggested using the dark cupboard under the stairs for developing his pictures, he spent more of his spare time in his "laboratory," as he called it, than anywhere else.

Jacob, on the other hand, loved magic. Every day he introduced to the family another of his sleight-of-hand tricks.

The house had a front yard and a back yard. The first night in their new home on Lytton Road, Benjamin brought home a little black puppy for the children, which gladdened their hearts. This was a *home* in every sense. They called the puppy Prince, and he soon became the pet of the family. Then a cat was added. Later, when eggs became scarce, Benjamin put up some chicken coops in the back yard, and a hen and 12 chicks were made welcome. With all this livestock to look after and spoil, there was plenty of diversion for the children.

Yente worked hard to care for her growing family. It seemed that whatever she touched was blessed. Soon her neighbors called her "Yente with the green thumb." They would bring sickly and dying plants to her, and she would nurse them, pat them, and talk to them, and soon they were alive with robust health. She planted potatoes and cabbage, and in a few months she was serving them to her family. Her chickens increased. Soon she set hens herself, and out of 12 eggs 12 chicks would come—not one spoiled. How wonderful life was. How good the Lord was to them.

The door of the big house at 34 Lytton Road was always open to guests. Hebrew Christians received an especially warm welcome, a good meal, and a spiritual blessing when they visited the Sitenhofs.

Among the Jewish believers who felt at home with the Sitenhof family were several young men in their 20s. They came from Poland and had no relatives in England. One was a bookbinder—a quiet, studious, learned young intellectual who had no home except with the Sitenhofs. One day he gathered the courage to ask Yente if he could live with them, and a small room on the third floor was made ready. He soon became like one of the family. He, too, did pretty well with the "bobbins" at night.

By the end of 1915 the zeppelins stopped coming. They were too slow and cumbersome and an easy mark for British guns and rifles. Now, instead of zeppelins, big, lumbering airplanes came day and night from across the English Channel. They would drop a few bombs and scurry back to France or Belgium.

These air raids became increasingly dangerous and destructive. As soon as the eerie warning of the sirens sounded, the children were brought downstairs and wrapped in blankets, for the open fireplace was the only means of heating the house. Mattresses were put under the table or under the stairs, and the family congregated in the hall of the basement, which was the living quarters. In the streets, policemen and special air raid wardens shouted, "Take cover! Take cover!"

When the bombs fell, windows were invariably smashed by the blast. On two occasions it was only by the grace of God that the family was not wiped out. During the air raids, which often lasted two or three hours, Lydia, who loved the Lord, put her fingers in her ears (to keep out the deafening sound) and prayed. Her faith was simple; she trusted in Him. Lydia never showed fear or panic like the little girl next door, who looked for pity all day because the bombs at night frightened her so much. When Lydia ran short of words to pray, she repeated the 23rd Psalm over and over again:

> The LORD is my shepherd; I shall not want . . . he leadeth me . . . though I walk through the valley of the shadow of death, I will fear no evil . . . Surely goodness and mercy shall follow me all the days of my life; and I will dwell in the house of the LORD forever.

In Her Tongue the Law of Kindness

Yente was busy keeping her family well fed and happy during the war years. When chicken feed was scarce, the younger children were sent to the market on Saturday morning to pick up the green outer leaves that had been trimmed off the cabbages. They would sometimes stagger home, each with two big bags full. As a reward they each received an extra egg.

But Yente made time to serve the Lord. The lady missionaries of the East End were always busy visiting poor and sick Jewish families, often arriving just in time to help at a childbirth and doing the most menial tasks. Yente joined in and worked right along with them, and she never went empty-handed. The most welcome gift was eggs from her own chickens, an extra blessing in the days when eggs were scarce and rationed. Yente always kept a dozen "reserved for the needy."

She was especially burdened for one Jewish family named Rosen who had seven young children. They had attended the services at the mission for a number of years, and although the father professed faith in the Lord, his life was not a testimony. Consequently, his wife and children often suffered from hunger and cold.

Yente was a ministering angel to this poor Jewish woman. Knowing that Esther Rosen still insisted on kosher cooking, Yente made it a point, when presenting one of her chickens to her, to have it killed by a *shocket*, the duly ordained and authorized Jewish butcher. This meant taking a live chicken on an hour-long trolley ride to the Jewish slaughter house. Often it was a rooster who usually kept the other passengers entertained by crowing all the way into town.

After the chicken was killed *kosher* style by the butcher, Yente had the job of plucking and preparing it according to the Jewish ritual. This required soaking the chicken for an hour in cold water, salting it on every side, and keeping it salted for a half hour so that the blood would flow down freely, for the children of Israel are forbidden to eat anything that contains blood. Then she put the chicken in a pot to boil, rolled the dough to make handmade noodles, scrubbed the floor, and washed the children. By that time the dinner was ready, and the children were waiting to be fed.

When Yente finished, it was usually late, and she was weary. As she worked, she spoke to Esther Rosen about the Lord, trying to explain to this simple Jewish woman that He loved and cared for her.

All Mrs. Rosen ever said was, "You, Mrs. Sitenhof, are my angel. What would we do without you?" Dishes washed, the apartment spic-and-span, the children in bed, Esther kissed good night, Yente at last took her leave and arrived home around midnight, blessedly tired. Thus she served the Lord faithfully and with a glad heart.

23

An Air Raid

I N 1916, with supplies of food becoming more limited every day, Yente was fully occupied trying to keep her family as well fed as possible. There were shortages of potatoes, the staple food, and margarine, to say nothing of butter.

For hours on end, Yente stood in line, and often, when at last her turn came, the supply had just run out. Disappointed and weary, she went home empty-handed. Rationing was introduced at last, although in an inadequate way. But at least there was a fairer distribution of available quantities.

As the war progressed, the air raids were more frequent and more violent. The airplanes came across the English Channel in squadrons like birds, and the humming of 20 or 30 engines high in the sky sent chills down people's backs as they scurried to take cover. One such raid was staged on a Saturday morning when housewives were out marketing. Yente had left the three girls home to do their chores while she took her place in the never-ending queues. Suddenly, as if from nowhere, a horde of planes was seen and heard. Police, mostly on horseback, appeared simultaneously and galloped up and down High Street shouting instructions to the people to hurry and take cover.

Yente, frenzied at the thought of her girls being home alone, disentangled herself from the crowd and turned on her heels for home, about ten blocks away. The scene about her was one of utter confusion. A policeman tried to grab her and push her into a doorway, but she freed herself crying, "My children, I must get home to my children."

Then the bombs started falling in the area. At every whistle of a bomb, she clutched the nearest lamppost and shut her eyes praying, "Lord bring me safely home; my children need me." At home fear gripped the three girls when they heard the whistle and "take cover," followed by the spine-chilling wailing of the sirens. Their mother was out in the street. They knew instinctively that she would rush home to them, bombs or no bombs, and the thought frightened them more than the terrifying explosions. They stood against the wall and, amid tears and anguished cries, prayed to God for their mother's safety. This was the worst raid they had experienced yet.

Outside, the antiaircraft guns in front of the house were shooting at the German planes. Each time a burst of shells was fired, it felt like everything for miles around had collapsed. The house rocked at its foundations.

Then out of the uproar came a cry. It reached the girls in the basement. It was their mother. "Lord you have saved me, you have saved my children, I thank you." With that she collapsed at the foot of the steps at the girls' feet.

Such memories last a lifetime. They are burned into the mind and heart. Turmoil, confusion, and destruction may be all around, but for the true believer there is a Shepherd who keeps His own through it all. Against such, hell itself shall not prevail.

The war dragged on interminably it seemed, leaving its mark and scars on the people. Benjamin worked hard all hours of the day and night—sometimes being sent on secret assignments for days at a time. He was thin and wan, as was Yente. And yet there was such peace in the home that it seemed like an oasis in a desert place. When the family was together for the evening meal and the time for evening devotions came, it seemed that the balm of Gilead was poured out in that little home, and Jesus Christ was in their midst.

In 1918, after Benjamin was exempted from military service for the third time due to the important government work he was doing, the hostility toward him on the part of the other men at work reached a point where it was not safe for him to be seen on the streets after dark. The situation was brought to the attention of the captain in charge of the plant, who guaranteed him safety while at work but shook his head when the question of safety after working hours was broached. The Lord, however, took care of Benjamin, and no harm came to him.

Armistice Day

November 11, 1918—Armistice day came as suddenly as the declaration of war had come. What a day of rejoicing it was. Bonfires were kindled in the streets, and fireworks were the order of the day and night, much to the delight of the younger Sitenhofs.

But as soon as darkness set in, Benjamin and Yente gathered their children around the table in front of the open fireplace, and the Word of God was studied and expounded by father. The Psalms were read, and praise and thanksgiving were offered to the Lord, while outside the drunken crowds continued all through the night paying homage, as it were, to the Devil himself, who had brought about this strife and bloodshed.

Let Glasgow Flourish

With the war over, Ernest felt the call to prepare himself for full-time service as a preacher of the Word of God. In 1919 he left for Glasgow, Scotland, where he studied for three years at the Bible Training Institute, an outstanding Christian institution preparing missionaries and preachers.

Glasgow was then a strong evangelical center. Its motto was, "Let Glasgow Flourish by the Preaching of the Gospel." Later, however, the motto was shortened to "Let Glasgow Flourish."

While a student, Ernest took a lively part in all Christian efforts and campaigns in Glasgow. He attended street meetings and gospel services in mission halls, putting his heart and soul into his witness for the Lord. Of course, Ernest's heart was especially among his Jewish brethren.

On Saturdays and Sundays he attended meetings in the Gorbels Cross district where most of the Jews were concentrated. Often he and others were treated with such *tokens of welcome* as rotten tomatoes, spoiled eggs, and similar expressions of *affection*. Nevertheless, the Lord had provided, even among these people seemingly impervious to the gospel, those who listened to the word of life and believed.

After the war, Benjamin's heart again turned to the mission field. The Bolshevik Revolution in Russia was raging, and he wondered about the outcome. Had his sisters and other relatives survived the bloodshed? He started praying, "Lord, there is always a great spiritual need after a war. Send me to a field of Thy choosing."

For three years Benjamin prayed for the Lord to thrust him out, and when, in 1921, the Irish Presbyterian Church gave him a call to go to Danzig, he was ready.

The free city of Danzig was a beautiful city of 350,000 people on the Baltic Sea. Bordered by Germany on one side and Poland on the other, it had a checkered past. A bone of contention between two rival nations, it had belonged to Poland and then to Germany. The people were mostly German, and German was the language spoken. When Germany lost the war, the League of Nations made Danzig a free city with its own senate and passports. As the revolution in Russia progressed, thousands of refugees, both Jews and Gentiles, fled through Poland to the free city of Danzig, where they were permitted to stay on the condition that they were not a burden to the state.

Many of these refugees were wealthy Jewish merchants, students, teachers, etc. The rich Jews brought with them their jewels and movable precious possessions, which they sold gradually, and managed to settle down in comfort. Some started businesses, some dealt on the stock exchange (often losing everything), and some lived or died on their gambling profits or losses at the well-known casino in nearby Zoppot, where roulette and other gambling games were allowed for all comers except Danzigers.

Then there were those refugees who were poor—people of all ages who had escaped the Communist revolution in Russia with their lives but sacrificed all else, some even their families. They were a confused, bewildered, motley group of people without homes, food, or work. Above all, they were spiritually stranded and adrift.

To these poor ones, rather than to the wealthy, Benjamin went as soon as he could get entry papers. He was peculiarly fitted to work in Danzig, for he was among his own people whose backgrounds he knew and understood. He could speak their languages—Russian, Polish, or German—and could minister to them in a singular way.

A Family Conference

When Benjamin received the call to minister in Danzig, a family conference took place. Yente and the children dreaded the thought of leaving the home they had acquired with such difficulty. But seeing the light in Benjamin's eyes, his joy and anticipation, they were caught up in the spirit of adventure for the Lord. It was decided that Benjamin would go first, since it was difficult to obtain passports for the entire family so soon after the war, and the family would follow in a year or so after he had established himself.

Benjamin felt the call so acutely that he did not even wait to take out a British passport, as was his right, but took a Polish passport, much to his regret later on.

Danzig was a three-day journey by train, and Benjamin stopped on the way to see David Fogel, his sister Dora, and their family in West Germany, from whom he had not heard since 1914.

To Yente, who had moved so often and given up one home after another, this meant just another move for the Lord, and she would make it willingly. But what about the children? Mary and Lydia would, of course, go with her. They were too young to leave. Betty was engaged to an Englishman and was to be married the following year. Ernest wanted to study for the ministry. Jack was undecided about his future. He was working as an apprentice in the same plant as his father, and he did not seem to want to leave. It was decided, therefore, that he would stay in England for a while and see if he could make it on his own.

The idea of being separated from the boys grieved Yente, for she knew how much they still needed her. And yet the call was there, and she had to answer it.

The one piece of furniture the Sitenhofs hated to part with was the piano, which had been purchased during the war years with contributions from every member of the family. That was the only piece that was sold, and the rest was given away— for all it was worth. Things—material things—did not fetter the Sitenhofs. They freed themselves easily of anything that might hinder their activities for the Lord. And, strangely enough, every time the Lord provided a nicer home, each one more beautiful than the last.

Benjamin patterned his life after that of the Apostle Paul, the greatest of all missionaries. He gave no thought to his personal comfort. He was on fire for the Lord, and his heart's desire and prayer for Israel was that they might be saved (Rom. 10:1).

Often Benjamin forgot altogether that he had a family; he was, with complete concentration, about his Father's business (Lk. 2:49). His family did not always understand his actions and complete abandon to the Lord's will, and they were often the cause of great anxiety. It takes much growth in the spirit to appreciate such devotion.

24

Danzig, Gateway to the West

AFTER BENJAMIN had worked in Danzig for a year, his sense of being where the Lord wanted him was more than confirmed. He surveyed the land and saw the low level of spirituality and the crying need for someone to bring the message of life to the human driftwood of that great port city. He threw himself heart and soul into the work. But it was an uphill struggle. Danzig, a city teeming with thousands of Jews, was without the gospel message. It was uncultivated soil full of thorns and thistles. To Benjamin it was a stirring challenge.

A cosmopolitan throng crowded the streets, hotels, restaurants, beaches, and gambling places. Danzig was a "free city" in more than one sense—it was a city of moral and spiritual decay.

Freight ships from all over the world docked in Danzig to pick up or discharge their cargoes. Danzig and later her rival, the newly built Polish port of Gdynia, were the links between the East and the West, between Russia and Poland, and the rest of the world. Here the Ukrainian refugees, who in the early 20s fled the Bolshevik regime by the thousands, were processed before being allowed to embark as immigrants to other countries. Here they were quarantined for a time like animals and waited their turn for shipment to the United States. Among these refugees were many Jews.

Benjamin ministered to those in the camps that were hastily set up to house the emigrants. Few had ever been out of their native country before and were confused and utterly lost in the strange, bewildering, cosmopolitan city. Benjamin distributed tracts and gospels in Yiddish, Polish, and German, and he ministered to their physical needs whenever he could. These poor lost souls learned to love Benjamin. Some of them wept bitterly when at last their time came to leave. Several confessed Jesus as their Messiah before boarding the boat.

What a sight it was to see the Ukrainian peasants and their Jewish companions board the ships with their pets, pots and pans, and other possessions flung over their shoulders, some weeping for fear of the big ocean they were to cross, some actually refusing to go at the last moment. Many took heart when Benjamin assured them that other people just like himself—people who loved the Messiah Jesus—would be at the other end of their journey to welcome them. The love he showed gave them assurance.

In September of 1922 Yente and the girls arrived in Danzig, and the boys remained in England. Elizabeth was to return to England the following year to be married to her English farmer. Benjamin had rented a furnished apartment for his family as a temporary home. It was located on the fourth floor of a building overlooking the Danzig prison, a somber and depressing location. Every time the "Black Maria" arrived at the gates with another load of people charged with various crimes, the girls ran to the windows and observed the proceedings in tears.

There were door-to-door beggars by the thousands. Most of the family's meals were shared with one or two strangers who were hungry. They were served on the stairs by Lydia, who delighted to feed them. She actually encouraged them to come again, and when they left, a tract or a gospel was handed to each one. Soon word got around in beggar circles, and many new *customers* appeared.

"Jerusalem" in Danzig

About that time the Irish Presbyterian Mission to the Jews decided to build a mission house, and Benjamin was asked to supervise the construction of the large five-story building, the first mission center to the Jews in the city of Danzig. It was a time of inflation, and the *gulden*, the currency of Danzig, dropped daily in value. By the time a man received his wages, his pay for one day was worth the cost of a loaf of bread. As a result, laborers refused to work unless they were paid daily or even hourly. But even so, many lost heart. What was the use of working for money that was not worth the paper on which it was printed? *Wechselstuben*, or *exchange rooms* as they were called, sprang up all over the city. Foreign currency, especially the English pound and the American dollar, were coveted above all else.

To the man in the street, life in Danzig was an endless battle for the next meal. Suicides were the order of the day. Danzig became a city of sin and corruption. "Let us eat and be merry for tomorrow we die" seemed to be the spirit of the hour.

Into the newly completed mission house, which was christened "Jerusalem," many new refugees came and received a welcome. Most of them were young men, stranded and destitute lads between the ages of 17 and 23, who were fleeing from various countries in Eastern Europe. Many came from Poland and Russia.

Danzig was a haven to thousands of these homeless young Jews. Some found a refuge and the Messiah at the "Mission House Jerusalem." A bookstore and an auditorium were on the first floor, apartments for missionaries on the second and third floors, and a home for destitute Jewish inquirers on the fourth and fifth floors.

In "Jerusalem" they received not only shelter and daily bread, but also the bread of life. They were encouraged to read the Bible and learn about the Messiah of Israel. In later years many of these people recalled with affection the blessings they enjoyed at the mission in the early 20s. Some eventually became missionaries to their own people.

Wedding Bells

In the summer of 1923 Betty returned to England to get married, and Yente and Lydia accompanied her. At the age of 22, Betty was a beautiful bride. Always quiet and often in a pensive mood, one could not penetrate her deeper feelings. She had experienced so much sadness in her young life and so little ease and happiness, that she was thrilled at the prospect of settling down in a home of her own in England. Her husband was a *gentleman farmer* and cattle dealer who came from a well-to-do Essex family of squires and landowners.

When the wedding was over, Yente and Lydia were heartbroken when the parting came and they had to go back to Danzig.

One of the homeless, friendless, newly converted Hebrew Christians who found her way to the "Mission House Jerusalem" in Danzig was Bronislava Jamaika, a Polish Jewess about 30 years of age. Because of her faith in the Messiah, Bronislava had been completely rejected by her family. She was welcomed into the Sitenhof household before the mission was officially opened and remained with them for over two years. During that time she became very attached to the family, but her favorite was Lydia. Unable to find employment in her own trade as a maker of artificial flowers, Bronislava helped in the home and made herself generally useful. Rejected and expelled by her own family, she felt alone and insecure. But with Yente to befriend her and help her grow spiritually, and with Mary and Lydia to keep her stepping, she learned to laugh again and was happy.

On Lydia's 16th birthday, Broni (as she was affectionately called) told her something about her background in Poland. She recalled how heartless her family had been when they discovered that she went to the mission, and how she had lost her job as a result. When Lydia, who was a sympathetic and good listener, asked Broni whether there were any others in her family who believed in the Messiah, she replied, "Yes, I have a cousin, 21 years old, who accepted Christ and was baptized. He is now studying at the University of Warsaw. It was through him that I first became interested in Christianity. He is such a fine young man, and it would be nice if you could meet him. Perhaps you would fall in love with him and marry him some day." "What is his name?" asked Lydia. "Victor" she replied, "Victor Buksbazen." The conversation was soon forgotten by Lydia, and the name did not even register in the young girl's mind.

Broni's dream was to spend the rest of her life with Lydia, who understood her so well, and her thoughts often dwelt on any opportunity that might make it possible.

"Lydia," she often said, "when you get married I will come and live with you and take care of your family for the rest of my life."

Cousin Victor was mentioned affectionately once or twice by Broni after that, but nothing she could devise brought him any closer to Danzig.

The German language was one of the great handicaps with which the girls had to contend. For several years during their early childhood they had spoken only German. But since they had lived in London, only English was spoken, especially during the war years. German was soon forgotten. How quickly children learn and then forget a language. Mary and Lydia now struggled to learn German again, but not hard enough. *Why learn German when so many Germans and some Danzigers speak some English or at least seem to understand it?* they reasoned. Many refugees planned, hoped, and dreamed of going to England or America some day and tried hard to learn English. "Speak to me in English," they said, eager to hear it spoken.

The girls' education in German was thus cut short, and Lydia decided to take a business course in shorthand and typing. But her progress was slow since she was not able to understand her German-speaking instructor.

After six months, her business course only half completed, Lydia found a position as private secretary to a lumber exporter. He thought it would enhance his business standing to introduce an English secretary to his customers. But his "English secretary" could neither write German letters nor take dictation in English well—certainly not his dictation. The English vocabulary of her boss consisted chiefly of "Good morning," "Good afternoon," "Have a cup of tea," and "Good business."

The "job" turned out to be that of errand girl, and no office work was involved. Lydia was sent out in all kinds of weather. In winter, when it was bitterly cold (sometimes 20 degrees below freezing), she was told to take letters, messages, and documents to banks, shipping houses, and customers. Sometimes she was sent to the docks to deliver shipping papers to boats. The docks and boats fascinated her. Benjamin was not happy that Lydia had gone to work before completing her education, but he knew it was one of the sacrifices a missionary must make if he wants his children with him in the field, and so he held his peace.

After three months of running around in the intense cold, Lydia left her first job and applied for a position at one of the Scandinavian shipping companies. She had little practice in English shorthand, but the night before the interview she went through her stenography textbook. The next day, in fear and trepidation, she was ushered into the office of Captain Burton, an Englishman who was looking for a secretary. Lydia was anxious to obtain this job, yet deep in her heart she knew how ill prepared she was for it.

Captain Burton looked at the slip of a girl—just 16, almost four years younger than any other girl in the big company—and smiled to himself. With long corkscrew curls dangling over her shoulders and a confident air (because she could at least speak English), she grasped the pencil and pad when he said he would give her a test. However, when she tried to read back the dictation, her lack of experience was evident. "Don't be discouraged little girl," Captain Burton told her. "You made a valiant effort. I love your spunk. Come back next year when you are 17 and have had a little more practice."

Her heart sank, and she fought to keep back her tears. "Captain Burton," she said, "please give me one more chance before next year. I'll come back in three days, and if I fail your test then, I will wait until next year. But I am sure I shall be satisfactory." Captain Burton patted her on the shoulder and with a wide grin said, "With that spirit I couldn't refuse you, but I don't for the life of me know how you will make it in three days."

That was the challenge Lydia needed. She ran home, got out her books, and made everyone who knew any English at all give her dictation, or at least talk to her while she wrote it in shorthand. Then she transcribed every word as best as she could. Every caller at the mission for the next three days was pressed into service, for that job meant more to her than anything else at the time. For three days Lydia neither ate nor slept, but when she returned for the test on Thursday of that week, to the amazement of the unbelieving Captain Burton, Lydia passed and got the position at Bergenske Baltic Transports, Ltd.

The company's headquarters was a five-story office building where Lydia mingled with Danes, Norwegians, Swedes, and Britishers. She could speak English all day long. She learned her work quickly and became so efficient that Captain Burton, who left the firm shortly thereafter to become an independent Lloyds of London agent, asked Lydia to be his secretary and work for him at a much increased salary. But nothing could tempt her to leave, not even the idea of doubling her salary. Money meant nothing to Lydia. The thought of the travel and adventure the shipping firm offered kept her there.

And travel opportunities soon came. By summer she was booked to go to London on a 1,500-ton cargo boat loaded with timber from the Baltic states. These freighters usually carried several passengers, all employees in the company offices. The pleasant five-day trip to London was a privilege reserved for valued employees only.

25

The Invisible Wall

THE FREE CITY OF DANZIG was definitely the crossroads of Eastern Europe. Emigrants flocked there in order to go on to better and freer countries. Young Jewish people, unable to enter colleges and universities in their anti-Semitic homelands, gathered in Danzig, where the atmosphere was more congenial and friendly.

And so it came to pass that one day Benjamin's sister Sima from Warsaw appeared in Danzig, bringing along several of her grown sons and daughters to explore the possibility of studying there. Benjamin was overjoyed to see his sister, whom he had not seen since his conversion 20 years before. She was married to a businessman, Aaron Goldberg, and was the mother of ten children.

Her older children were already engineers and doctors, and some of the younger ones were students at the University of Warsaw. Sima was very friendly toward Benjamin. She said, "Let us just remember that you are my brother and I am your sister, and we will get along fine. Come and see us in Warsaw, and bring your family along. You will be more than welcome."

One day Benjamin went out to visit his sister and brother-in-law in their cultured and comfortable home in Warsaw. It was a hospitable home, open to one and all, and the younger set of Jewish intelligentsia often gathered there. This was Benjamin's natural environment—comfortable, cultured, and gay. The Goldbergs received him with open arms, but before long he felt out of place. He could not feel at home where Christ was not loved. He felt the conflict between divided loyalties, between his dear ones according to the flesh and his faith.

Mary and Lydia, who accompanied their father to meet their cousins, felt strange in this intensely Jewish atmosphere. They could not understand Polish, which was spoken in the Goldberg home, and so a smattering of German had to do as a means of communication.

University students, doctors, engineers, and ardent Zionists often visited the Goldberg home. Zionism among the Jews in the early 20s was in full blossom. It was the hope of Israel, persecuted, despised, and discriminated against in Europe. In the Goldberg home Zionism was the family religion.

The Sitenhof girls knew little about the Zionist movement and its strong effect on Jewish thinking and feeling. To them the future of the Jews was the divine plan for Israel according to the Scriptures. The ardent spirit of Jewish nationalism and Zionism was strange and bewildering. The girls listened carefully, and the fervent spirit of these young people pervaded their hearts. Then they heard the Jewish national anthem, Hatikvah, the Hope:

> So long as the Jewish heart Beats in a Jewish breast And Jewish eyes with longing gaze Toward Zion in the east; So long our Hope shall never perish, The ancient Hope and immortal, Yet to be a people free In Zion's land and in Jerusalem.

The fervent yearning and intensity of this song could not help but touch their hearts. They longed for God to restore the Holy Land to His scattered people. A new world was opened to them, and they were caught up in the enthusiasm that their numerous cousins and friends displayed.

Lydia's mind was in a turmoil. She was a faithful witness and follower of the Lord Jesus Christ and knew she must take a stand for Him, but this was unpleasant and unwelcome to the Goldberg family. Mary, in order not to offend, remained quiet on the subject. But Lydia spoke up, in spite of the fact that she was told by her cousins to keep her religion to herself. This made Lydia the least popular with the cousins. They liked her and her sister, but they wanted none of the strange religious ideas that Lydia freely voiced.

It was a delicate situation with the unbelieving relatives. They wanted to enjoy the companionship of their aunt, uncle, and cousins from England, and there was a mutual attraction between them, but there was a strong barrier at the same time. Lydia often thought of the verse, "I came not to send peace, but a sword" (Mt. 10:34).

In the early spring of 1925 Elizabeth, who lived in England, gave birth to her first child, a son, little Dick. Betty was extremely busy with her duties on the farm and her family, so she asked Lydia to come from Danzig and stay with her for a while. Lydia was only too glad to do so.

To Lydia, England, where she had lived for the first seven years of her school life and where she had blossomed from childhood into young womanhood, meant home. She longed for her family to be back with her in England. She often prayed that the Lord would bring them back, if He saw fit, and give her father a mission field at home. London was teeming with Jews. Why couldn't he be a witness to them?

In her childlike faith, she believed the Lord would answer her prayer. She kept busy on the farm, feeding the chickens, looking after the baby, and helping with the housework. Time passed rapidly; but she longed for her family, especially her mother.

A Prayer Answered

Around that time the International Hebrew-Christian Alliance was founded in London. The first conference was to take place in London in 1926. Lydia was thrilled when she received a letter from Danzig saying her father and mother were planning to attend that conference and that her father had accepted a call to work in London under the London City Mission. Lydia was sure the Lord had answered her prayers.

A deep sense of gratitude pervaded her being. Thank God, now the family would be together again. No longer would the boys have to live by themselves; they would live in their own home with their parents. Truly the Lord was good.

Ernest and Jack, however, were both eager to study for the ministry. Some Christian friends from America, who were guests in the newly established Sitenhof home, urged the boys to come to America, where they would have the opportunity to work their way through college. In England, any kind of education was prohibitive at that time. Only the well-to-do could afford a college education.

Off to Moody

In the spring of 1926 Ernest left for Chicago to enter Moody Bible Institute. A few months later Jack too was on his way to Chicago, aboard the good ship Leviathan, headed for Moody. Yente was heavyhearted on parting with her dear ones, but she realized it meant a future in the service of the Lord, and she was grateful for the opportunities that came their way.

Lydia was in her element in London. She confidently went out looking for office work. With her partial knowledge of German, she was able to obtain a position in a shipping firm in London. Mary worked as a saleslady in a store. Soon the Sitenhofs settled down to a quiet life, and Betty's son Dick was the delight of the whole family.

The Barbican Mission to the Jews in London was, at the time, establishing an Inquirers' Home and School in the north of London for young Jewish converts. Benjamin was askeα to take charge. He seemed to be particularly suited for this work. Again the family moved, this time to a large house in the north of London. Soon the home was filled with young men who came from all parts of Europe, including the Danzig Mission in Poland. Under the able teaching of Benjamin, some of them were prepared for future training as missionaries.

The next five years were busy ones in the Sitenhof home. When a letter came from the boys in America, it was truly a red-letter day for the whole family. They wrote cheerful letters. They were working hard at college and maintained themselves by doing all kinds of work between their study periods. Jack was, in turn, a park sweeper, an elevator boy, a waiter, and, on occasion, a magician. Magic tricks were his specialty, and he was quite popular at commencement exercises in various schools, where he combined his magic with a Christian message. On Sundays both Ernest and Jack preached in churches, sometimes out in the country. In this way they gained experience in the ministry.

A few years later the Inquirers' Home was closed, and Benjamin worked among the Jewish people in the East End of London, visiting, speaking in the open air, and preaching the gospel faithfully and untiringly.

Mary had by this time started a small gown shop and was kept busy. Lydia had worked for several firms and gained much experience in office routine. Lydia and her mother were joined together by deep affection and friendship. She knew how much her mother missed the boys, and she tried to make up for the loss, at least in part.

Benjamin's heart, however, was still burdened for Danzig. There were so many missionaries in London who could do his work, but there were few or none in Danzig. He therefore returned to Danzig in 1931, without the backing of any mission board, trusting the Lord to provide. Lydia had secured a good job and was able to support her mother if necessary. The call to Danzig was so definite and irresistible that none of the family could object. Benjamin's heart was on the foreign mission field. In the ensuing years he often went hungry and was unable to pay the rent for a small room. Many times his converts shared with him a loaf of bread or a pot of soup. Material things meant little to Benjamin. He had the true spirit of the early disciples of the Savior. He was not concerned about clothing, food, or where he would sleep. He simply went forth in faith.

The years of stress and strain had left their mark on Yente, who now suffered with rheumatism. Yet they were happy years.

Lydia did her utmost to provide her mother with every comfort. On weekends Betty came from the farm bearing gifts of eggs, butter, cream, and vegetables. Betty's husband was a sickly man, and the burden of her small family fell upon her shoulders. But she was of the stock that weathers storms bravely. She was faithful and strong.

By now Lydia was secretary to a leather merchant in Bermondsey, London. He was a German Jew who looked upon her as his right arm. He introduced her to customers saying, "She says she is a Jewess who believes in the Messiah. I say she is a Goy, for she does not keep our holidays. But whatever she is, I would entrust her with all I have and more, for she is faithful—the best secretary I have ever had." Her business connections gave Lydia many opportunities to witness to her Jewish customers. And, strangely enough, she was respected by them as a Christian.

Ernest was eventually ordained in California as a minister of the gospel and returned to England. The *unprodigal* son came home, and the joy was great. He was offered the pastorate of St. Columba Church in Walthamstow, London. A year later his bride-to-be, Ella, arrived, and they were married in Ernest's church. Ella Grauer was from French-German descent. Her father David was a pioneer who went to California before the turn of the century. He worked hard building an orange farm and a home for his growing family and, incidentally, helped transform the wasteland of Southern California into the thriving province which it later became.

Ella was raised in a deeply Christian atmosphere and had a God-given love and burden for the Jews. As a young girl she went to the Bible Institute of Los Angeles, and during her student years she worked closely with Dr. Immanuel Gittell in a Jewish mission. It was there that she met Ernest, and they fell in love.

But now clouds—dark, angry, and low hanging—were gathering over Europe and the entire world. An evil maniac named Adolf Hitler came into power in Germany. Events were moving rapidly to an awesome climax.

26

The Hebrews of Hutton

A FTER ERNEST AND ELLA were married, they and Lydia purchased a bungalow in the country for their mother. They felt it was time Yente had a place of her own, and Whitby Moor, as they called the red brick bungalow in Hutton, Essex, was the home in which she spent the happiest years of her life.

Hutton was a peaceful hamlet removed from the noise and rush of the big city, and yet near enough for Lydia to commute to work in London, just a half hour away by the express train. In the evening Lydia would come home worn out from work, but the peace and quiet of the country were so invigorating and soothing that in the morning she felt fresh as a daisy, ready to catch the express to London again.

Those precious memories would always linger in Lydia's heart. There was the soft twilight of those balmy summer evenings as she sat on the veranda with her mother after a day in the city and heard the hoot of the owl and the chirping of the cricket, smelled the newly cut grass, so pungent it was almost intoxicating, saw the full moon rise over the meadow at the end of the garden throwing a path of light directly at them, heard the cows mooing in the distance, and the echo coming back, and enjoyed the silence of the summer night softly enfolding them and making them lift up their heads to Heaven and thank Him who made all things and made them well.

The flowers Yente grew were so varied and colorful and the lawns so green that one was reminded of a picture postcard of an old English garden with roses around the door. The sweet peas grew up the sides of the veranda in great profusion, and their scent, mixed with that of the wallflowers growing in abundance nearby, made one stagger at times.

In the eight years they lived at Whitby Moor, nothing ever became commonplace to Lydia or Yente, nothing was ever taken for granted. Every morning the heavy dew clinging to the lawns and flowers and the scent of the carnations and roses that greeted their nostrils through the always-open windows thrilled them anew. Here indeed was rest from the bustling world. Here Yente's dream came true.

Yente's love for flowers, the warm smile she always had for her neighbors, and her love for children became proverbial in the hamlet. The Sitenhofs were considered a different kind of people and nicknamed, not without affection, the "Hebrews of Hutton."

The Man with the Funny Mustache Takes Over

Everything was so peaceful and happy in Whitby Moor. Yente tended to her flowers—hoed, seeded, sowed, and lovingly nursed those plants that were not doing well, until they too looked happy and smiling.

But on April 30, 1933, darkness descended upon the Jews of the world, and not only on the Jews but on all mankind. Adolf Schicklgruber Hitler became Chancellor of Germany. Hitler, born in a little village on the Austrian-German border, was the son of a petty government official who, up to the age of 35, went by the name of Alois Schicklgruber. Hitler was a soldier in the Austrian army in the First World War, and he came home from the war embittered, unemployed, and frustrated.

Germany was a defeated and humiliated nation, suffering poverty, depression, and general demoralization. As always, the Jews became the scapegoat for their frustrations and unfulfilled desires for conquest and enrichment.

The little corporal brooded over his personal and national misfortune and mingled with similar, embittered veterans. Their philosophy was a mixture of hatred for democracy, the Western Allies, and, above all, the Jews. Hitler, with his hysterical oratory, soon became their spokesman and leader. It was one of those remarkable instances in history when a neurotic, half-crazed demagogue was able to personify and give expression to all the secretly nurtured or openly expressed desires and hatreds of a great nation.

His half-literate book, *Mein Kampf*, setting forth his "gospel" of hatred and his blueprint for world conquest, was forced upon the German people as their new *Bible*. Hitler, his book *Mein Kampf*, and violent threats against the world in general and the Jews in particular were brushed aside or even laughed away as things not to be taken seriously. When the world realized its mortal peril, it was too late.

The only statesman who, in those darkening years, recognized the real menace of Hitler and his gangsters was Winston Churchill. He warned England and the world of the wrath to come. But his was "a voice crying in the wilderness" of indifference or intimidated leaders. For his pains, Churchill was rebuffed and rebuked until it was too late.

Winston Churchill later described Adolf Hitler as "a bloodthirsty guttersnipe, a monster of wickedness, insatiable in his lust for blood and plunder."

The men around Hitler—the Goehrings and the Goebbels— looked upon him as or pretended to believe that he was the "messiah" of the German people, a god of the ancient German Valhalla, the seat of bloodthirsty, mythological deities and cruel heroes. In the words of his lieutenant and mouthpiece, Joseph Goebbels, the destiny of Hitler was "to unchain volcanic passions, to arouse outbreaks of fury, to set masses of men on the march, and to organize hate and suspicion, with ice-cold calculation."

And the man with the unruly forelock, the dark smidgen of hair for a mustache, and the coarse voice did exactly that. A nation entrusted her honor and future to a demon-possessed man.

His main object of hate was the Jew, whom, like his predecessor Haman, he vowed to exterminate altogether. But for the grace of God, he came very close to achieving his satanic purpose.

Yente sat at her radio listening to the mad rantings of this evil man who made no secret of his intention to destroy the Jews. She suffered inwardly more than she showed. Every time she heard him speak, it was like a knife piercing her heart. Yes, she "looked for a city which hath foundations, whose builder and maker is God" (Heb. 11:10). And here was a wretched man claiming to be the "savior" and "builder" of the German people. Yente often said to Lydia, "Doesn't he know that without God he can only lose?"

She meditated and read her Bible daily and was deeply troubled in spirit because of the threats that were constantly flung at her people in a voice more venomous with hatred than the world had ever heard. Those were hard days for Yente. Her heart was torn for the plight of her brethren in Germany.

Early in 1935 Lydia tired of office work and decided to venture into another field on her own. She rented a small dress shop in Muswell Hill in the north of London, and although she started with very little capital, by May of that year she was doing very well.

Never having worked in sales before, people (and Lydia herself) were amazed to discover that she had unusual sales ability. Within three months she established such a good reputation that wholesalers were eager to give her credit. She was always prompt in paying her bills.

Handy with a needle and a sewing machine, she made all alterations of coats, suits, and dresses herself, thus cutting expenses. There were no complaints; satisfied customers came back again and again. This discovery of a *new* Lydia gave her added confidence. Her turnover increased every month by one hundred per cent.

In the spring of 1935 Lydia was introduced to a young man at the home of a Hebrew-Christian friend, Rev. Jacob Peltz, who at the time was secretary for the International Hebrew-Christian Alliance in London. Lydia and her sister Mary had been invited to a Sunday afternoon tea. On seeing the young minister, she remarked to her sister that he reminded her of Broni in Danzig. "Do you mean Bronislava Jamaika?" the young man asked. "Yes, how did you guess I meant her?" Lydia inquired. "Because," he answered, "Bronislava Jamaika is my second cousin."

So here was the Victor Buksbazen dear Broni had mentioned to Lydia 12 years before. How strange and inscrutable are the ways of God! Broni's cousin was now a young, ordained minister of the gospel, serving as a missionary to the Jews in Cracow, Poland, on a deputation tour in England. And Lydia, of all people, met him. Could it be other than the hand of God bringing these two people together?

They were mutually drawn to each other. In fact, when they first saw each other they knew that something very important had happened in their lives.

When Victor and Lydia met a second time three weeks later, he proposed marriage. At first she was not able to say yes, wanting to know more clearly the Lord's will in the matter. By the time she was ready to give a definite answer, many things had happened in the world, as well as in her own life. Both she and Victor went through the shadows during that time.

There were many lessons Lydia had to learn before the Lord could use her. Above all, she had to stand the test of suffering and grief. It is in this way that the Lord prepares those He uses for His purposes. He breaks them, melts them, molds them, and when the test is over, He fills them, if they are willing, with the Holy Spirit, and uses them to glorify Himself. But without the fire there can be no refining.

In August of 1935, having spent three months in England, Victor went back to his mission station in Cracow, where the

Lord was using him in the gospel witness to the Jews. Cracow was the ancient capital of Poland and had a thousand-year history—as old as Poland herself. At the end of the 18th century Poland was partitioned by her three rapacious neighbors into three parts. Cracow became the main city in Austrian Poland and the stronghold of orthodox Jewry.

It was a common sight to see long-bearded Jews with side curls, dressed in fur hats, long black coats, white socks, and knee breeches, walking to or from the synagogue and places of rabbinical learning. Missionaries from England had been carrying on a gospel witness among the Jews of Cracow for nearly a hundred years, and many Jews were saved. But every time a missionary passed away or retired, there was a lapse of several years in the ministry, and the small flock of believers was scattered.

When Victor was ordained to the gospel ministry, he was sent to revive the work in Cracow. The beginnings were very difficult and discouraging. But, as in other places, there were many Jews, especially among the younger generation, who were spiritually hungry and looking for food that would satisfy their souls. The preaching of the gospel opened up a new world—a gateway to a new life.

Jacob's Return

Jacob, who spent a number of years in the United States, studying at Moody Bible Institute and other Christian institutions, had by now completed his education and was ordained as a minister of the gospel. He decided to return home to his beloved mother and his family circle.

With him came a young friend named Roger Derby. Both Jack and Ernest, while students in America, met the Christian family of Mr. and Mrs. Lewis Derby of Minneapolis. The Derbys were true lovers of God's people and put their heart and soul into the cause of befriending the Jewish people, especially Christian Jews. People referred to their home as the "Hebrew-Christian Hotel."

Jack and Ernest found a home away from home, and Mrs. Derby was a mother to them in the absence of their own mother. Now Roger, a student of music, came to England with Jack to continue his musical studies. The Sitenhofs, especially Yente, were excited at the thought of having Jack home again. Now her happiness would be complete with her two sons back home and the whole family together.

Finally, in the early fall of 1935, Jack arrived in England. The whole family, except Benjamin who was still in Danzig, waited at Waterloo Station to greet him and his American friend. It had been nine years since they had been together, and it was a joyful reunion. Yente was happy, and her heart was full of praise and thanksgiving.

Christmas that year was a memorable one. The whole family gathered together at Whitby Moor to celebrate the Lord's birth. The little bungalow was full to overflowing. Fires burned cheerfully in the open grates of all the rooms. Hearts were happy to be together again, and voices were united in Christmas carols. The Lord was good to the Sitenhof family. The only cloud on their horizon was the one of hatred for the Jewish people hanging over Europe.

Jack was a powerful preacher—an orator for the Lord. He had studied long and hard in the United States, and now he was taking a rest and thoroughly enjoying the best home the Sitenhofs had ever had. Yente's cup was full and overflowing. She had both her sons with her again, and the future of the well-favored and popular Jack seemed to be especially bright and promising.

But "my thoughts are not your thoughts, neither are your ways my ways, saith the LORD" (Isa. 55:8). When the sun smiles down on green meadows and gardens in bloom, who gives a thought to the raging storm that may soon bring grief and suffering in its wake?

Lydia, the Seller of Purple

With the coming of Hitler, Jewish life and property in Germany underwent a complete devaluation. In fact, these commodities lost almost all value. Those Jews who were not interned in concentration camps or murdered outright were frantic to leave Germany. Those were days when a visa to a country outside the grasp of Hitler often meant a visa to life; its refusal, a sentence to death.

At that time a Jewish businessman named Hermann Silber, a merchant of printed silks and rayons, came to London with some of his capital, which he had somehow managed to get out of Germany. Anxious to set himself up in business, he made contacts with his business associates, inquiring for a person who could speak both German and English fluently and help him become established in England. Lydia Sitenhof was recommended as a most trustworthy and capable person.

When Mr. Silber approached Lydia, she did not want to accept his offer because she was happy in her own little business venture. But he opened his heart to her, telling her how badly he needed her help. He was a stranger in a strange land, and unless she were willing to help him, his future and that of his family would be in jeopardy. Mr. Silber persisted and would not take no for an answer. He came daily to her store to plead with her.

When Lydia said, "Herr Silber, I do not know anything about your business or your trade," he answered, "My dear young lady, anybody with common sense can learn a trade. But character, honesty, loyalty—these are gifts of God, and He has blessed you with them."

Lydia sought guidance and finally accepted Mr. Silber's offer, and he was very generous with her. He not only bought out her business, but he also offered her a more than adequate salary, the highest she ever earned in her life.

Strange, she thought. *Here is a Jewish man who knows I am a Jewish Christian, and yet, in spite of all his ingrained prejudices, he is willing to entrust me with his fortune and future.* Jewish people often take a negative stand against Christianity while deeply appreciating the fruit of the Spirit of Christ, an unconscious tribute to the greatest Molder and Maker of character.

The next day Mr. Silber and Lydia went to a bank, opened a deposit account, and rented a safe deposit box. When the manager asked Mr. Silber in whose name he wished to establish the account, he replied, "In the name of this young lady, Miss Lydia Sitenhof." "How much do you wish to deposit?" "Five thousand pounds for a start" [the equivalent of about $25,000]. "Do you know her well enough to entrust such a sum to her?" the manager inquired "Oh, yes," he replied, "I would entrust her with everything I have."

Mr. Silber handed over to Lydia the detailed instructions of his business, instructions that were the apple of his eye because they represented the entire basis for his future. Lydia was deeply moved by the confidence shown in her by a man she hardly knew. Mr. Silber had to rush back to Germany to attend to his business at the other end, but he promised to return in a week.

Lydia set to work with all her might. First she rented spacious offices and showrooms to display the goods her boss sent from Germany. Then she went into the details of her new duties. Every piece of silk had its basic price, transport price, and custom and income factor to be worked out exactly, and the thousands of different figures had to be at her fingertips. A German calculator was a great help. It was a mechanical wonder simplifying calculations in a marvelous way.

Then she employed a staff of traveling salesmen and office clerks. Mr. Silber's absence for "one week" was stretched into three months. When he came back, Lydia had hired the warehouse and office staff, the salesmen were busy getting new customers, the goods were in circulation, and the new enterprise was running smoothly—a going concern.

Benjamin Comes Home

In the meantime, Benjamin was in Danzig working among the Jewish people, seeking to comfort and help his little flock, which was exposed to the consuming hatred of the rising Nazi power. He stayed with them as long as he could, but his days in Danzig were numbered.

One day he was ordered to leave Danzig within 36 hours. There was no room under Hitler for the preaching of the gospel to the Jews, so Benjamin returned to London.

By this time England had become a haven of refuge to thousands of Jews fleeing from Hitler. Refugees from Germany, Austria, and Eastern Europe were pouring in daily, escaping Hitler's clutches. These people, in their suffering and bewilderment, were especially open to the claims of the gospel; their hearts were hungry for friendship and compassion.

Benjamin, always eager to witness to his beloved people, began a gospel ministry in Brighton, Sussex. On the southern coast of England, Brighton was within easy reach of London and was the hub of a cluster of seashore towns and resorts. Nearby were Hove, Worthing, Shoreham, Lancing, and many other towns. Each had a considerable number of Jewish people with few people to tell them about the Savior in their hour of need.

Benjamin knew these people from his previous life and service among them in Europe. He understood them, not only because he could speak their various languages, but also because he understood the unspoken language of their fears and woes, their hopes and yearnings. Soon Benjamin's mission in Brighton became the center of Christian witness and compassion.

27

The Isle of Man

PEERING AROUND THE CORNER was yet another time of trial for the Sitenhof family.

Jack was invited to candidate at a church in the town of Ramsey on the Isle of Man. He made an excellent impression on the congregation, and they decided unanimously to extend a call to him to become their pastor. Jack liked the church. Mr. Quilliam, one of the elders who was especially interested in the young pastor, took him around in his little Austin and introduced him to the mayor of the city and all the personalities of the island.

It was a beautiful island with deep, stormy bays and lovely beaches, hills, and hamlets. It dated back to ancient days and was inhabited by quaint but very friendly people. From the northern tip of the island Jack looked across the water and saw three ancient lands: Scotland to the north, England to the east, and the Emerald Isle called Ireland to the west.

Jack thrilled at the thought of his future ministry as a pastor. He was to preach his first sermon on Good Friday. To honor the new pastor and extend their goodwill, all the churches in Ramsey decided to hold a joint service with Jack Sitenhof bringing the message.

Lydia, who had had a successful but hard winter, planned to spend the Easter vacation on the isle. When she set out, the whole world looked perfect to her. The spring flowers seemed to be smiling especially at her. Life was wonderful indeed. She traveled at night, sitting on the deck of the boat as it crossed the Irish channel on its way to the island. Lydia was happy for her brother and glad at the prospect of a few days rest for herself on the isle that Jack had described as "a little bit of Heaven." When she left London, Mr. Silber encouraged her to stay a few days longer for a well-earned rest.

But instead of rest, grief waited to greet her. Lydia naturally expected her brother to meet the boat in Douglas, the port city and capital of the Isle of Man. When he was nowhere to be seen, she did not think too much about it but gathered her luggage and boarded the bus to Ramsey. It was a beautiful ride along the coastline, high on the cliffs above the sea. Its beauty defied description—rugged, stern, majestic. It was so breathtaking that Lydia almost forgot to alight at the address Jack had given her.

Then a sense of foreboding filled her heart. When her hand touched the knocker of the door, she knew all was not well. Something had happened to her brother in the seven days since he had left home. At her knock, Jack came downstairs. It was only 7 o'clock in the morning, and he was dressed in a robe, but when she saw his troubled countenance, she knew that something terrible had happened, and she was rooted to the spot.

Pulling herself together, she followed him up to his room. Not a word was spoken between them, not even the greeting Lydia had visualized so often during the night on board the boat. It became obvious to her that Jack was suffering a nervous breakdown. She spoke lovingly and tried to reason with him Even before she took her coat off, she got down on her knees with her brother and cried out to the Lord to take over. Then a calm took possession of her, a resolute calm that was the Lord's answer to her prayer. She acted quickly. It was Wednesday.

A meeting of the church session was called, and another preacher was secured for Good Friday. Lydia telephoned

London that she was flying back the next day with Jack. All at once, in the twinkling of an eye, it seemed that the world, which had looked so pleasant and serene the day before, had become a valley full of tears and grief. Lydia chartered a small plane, and by noon the next day, in brilliant sunlight, they were winging their way back home.

Is this a dream? Lydia wondered. Or perhaps it was a nightmare that would disappear just as the coastline of the Isle of Man was disappearing down below. Perhaps she would awaken to a reality sweeter than this ghoulish presence. "Oh, Lord, give us your strength, come to our aid, for there is no one else who can help us," Lydia prayed.

Yente's grief and heartache at the sudden turn of events were very deep. Doctors and specialists were consulted. Jack seemed to flounder in waves of distress. One day he seemed well, but by the next morning deep gloom had swept over him, and he was not himself. The pattern continued. It was a time of grief for the Sitenhof family, but the prayers offered for Jack were answered.

Lydia, who was earning more money than any of the other members of the family, gladly assumed the burden of the medical bills that were piling up. Even before the darkness of sorrow had set in, the Lord had provided help. What a blessing Lydia's position with Mr. Silber turned out to be for the entire family. Those who have not gone through the agony of waiting for a loved one to recover from such an illness cannot know the sorrow and despair associated with such an experience.

When a wholesome smile returned to the friendly face of brother Jack, it seemed that the Lord had smiled again upon the sorely tired family.

While Jack was recovering from his illness, Victor Buksbazen was involved in a horse cart accident in Poland. He was visiting friends in the country near Cracow, and as they were driving back to the city, the horse became frightened on the downgrade of a steep hill and spilled all the passengers along the highway. Victor was picked up by an ambulance having suffered a serious compound fracture of his left leg. A few days later a crisis set in, and his life was in the balance.

After five months in a hospital ward, lying on his back in one position, his leg in a cast, he was finally dismissed on crutches. Lydia at that time was going through the depths of despair with her beloved brother in England but was looking to the Lord to heal him, while at the same time Victor was in a Cracow hospital threatened with the amputation of his left leg. Thus the Lord teaches His children to remain humble and close to Him. When we think we are *sitting on top of the world,* He whispers to us to come sit by Him and learn patience and long-suffering. Through it all, He draws us closer to Himself.

At the same time, the war clouds in Europe were black and ominous. The persecution of the Jews was proceeding according to plan. By now Lydia had worked up a lucrative business for her employer in England and a substantial export business. From 8:00 a.m. to midnight she could be found working in the office. But the work and the burden of her brother's illness weighed heavily upon her. She asked the Lord for guidance, and it seemed that He spoke to her in a very definite way.

By the spring of 1937 Jack was well on his way to a good recovery. Now Lydia felt an urge to see Victor, after his accident, to discuss their future. He was anxious for her to live in Poland, and she was just as anxious not to do so for a number of reasons. Knowing the political situation, and especially the plight of the Jews of Europe under Hitler, Lydia felt as if a strong hand were holding her back, warning her not to live in Poland.

What then? How could two people be together and yet not live in the same country? But the Lord had laid His own plans for the future of His children. The pattern was taking shape. "How unsearchable are his judgments, and his ways past finding out!" (Rom. 11:33). During the same week Lydia was visiting Cracow, the General Secretary of the British Jews Society, under whom Victor was working in Cracow, was making his biannual visit to Poland, and the problem was discussed with him. After praying together about the situation, he decided that it would be wise at that time to call Victor to deputation work in Britain.

By August of 1937 Lydia and Victor were engaged to be married. As if by a miracle, and against his own will, Victor was snatched from the fury of Hitler's horror camps and gas chambers in which all of his relatives, including his mother, sisters, and other dear ones, perished.

Victor and Lydia were married on December 21, 1937, in St. Colomba Presbyterian Church, Walthamstow, of which Ernest Sitenhof was pastor. It was a memorable occasion, and Jack had recovered so well that, at his request, he escorted the bride to the altar.

Even Mr. Silber, who was overjoyed that he was not losing his business manager, came to the church and the reception. Churches in England are not heated, and consequently he caught cold and was in bed with pneumonia for weeks, but he always said he never regretted attending, as he was deeply impressed by the simple Christian ceremony.

Victor's work now consisted of preaching on behalf of the Jewish missionary work in various churches in England, Wales, and Ireland. Soon after his marriage, he embarked on a preaching tour that kept him away for three weeks. Lydia was, therefore, able to continue her work. They lived near Hampstead Heath in London, and in the evenings when Victor was home, they rambled over the Heath, taking long walks to picturesque old spots around Hampstead.

The Witches' Night

In February 1938 Lydia was asked to make a business trip to Germany, to serve two of the largest Australian buyers of German fabrics. Her ability to speak German and English fluently was a great asset in selling goods to the customers from England and overseas who could not speak German. Thus she found herself on a dull February day in a hotel in Krefeld, Germany, where she was to meet her Australian customers and take them to her company's warehouse in Cologne.

But the next 24 hours brought some terrifying experiences. It was the first day of the traditional *Fasching* (the equivalent of Mardi Gras or carnival). All day, as she waited and rested, people came and went. The excitement in the streets, cafes, and hotel lobby was rising with every hour. There was to be a *special* anti-Semitic display, and every one, young and old alike, was going to honor Hitler on that night in the way that would please him most. Lydia wisely stayed in her room and, behind drawn curtains, watched the parade assemble.

She locked her door from the inside since she feared trouble. And then the *fun* started. Large torches were lit, and a grotesque procession of people, intoxicated with liquor and hate propaganda, started up the street. She watched with bated breath. What were they carrying? She looked more intently and realized the gruesomeness of the situation. Great caricatures and stuffed, life-size dummies of such well-known Jews as Bernard Baruch, Sigmund Freud, Leon Blum, Albert Einstein, and others had been made. Their features were exaggerated in the most fantastic way with foot-long noses, huge ears, and big feet.

The effigies were being carried on long poles through the main street to the accompaniment of the raucous voices of Hitler's "leaders" singing despicable anti-Semitic songs such as the infamous "Horst-Wessel," which began with the words, "When Jewish blood from the knife spurts, Things will go much better for us."

After each song, roared by multitudes of drunken people, there were great shouts of "Down with the Jews. Let's kill them all. Let's burn them all." Then huge bonfires were started in the main street at intervals of about one hundred yards, and the effigies were burned. The fires were then fed with the looted contents of nearby Jewish homes. This was the "superior race" that Hitler wanted to set free from the Jews.

While the drunken hordes were reveling and merrymaking, the chief object of which was to revile and deride the Jews, the God of Israel looked down and saw the venom and contempt poured out upon His people and held their mockers in derision. "He who sitteth in the heavens shall laugh; the Lord shall have them in derision. Then shall he speak unto them in his wrath, and vex them in his great displeasure" (Ps. 2:4-5).

A little over a year later God did speak to these people in His wrath and vexed them in His great displeasure. Seven years later, in 1945, the Reich that Hitler built, which was to endure for a thousand years, lay in ruins, and beneath the rubble of a bunker in Berlin its evil founder—the man with the unruly strand of hair and funny mustache, Adolf Hitler—lay dead.

In 1948 the people of Germany again celebrated their traditional *Fasching* night. But then, instead of the hideous caricatures of famous Jews, the crowds carried life-size dummies of Hitler, Goering, Goebbels, and the demonic Streicher, the archenemy and maligner of the Jews. Then their effigies were burned in the streets of Cologne and other German cities.

Thus the God of Israel had the last laugh. As God said to Abraham, "I will bless them that bless thee, and curse him that curseth thee" (Gen. 12:3).

Lydia watched this dreadful scene from behind the draperies, fearing she would be seen and the mob would come for her. Outside her door crowds of people were milling around. There were hundreds more downstairs, in the halls, and on the stairs, all drinking and singing the vilest anti-Semitic songs she had ever heard. When she attempted to order food by telephone, she was told to go down to the dining room and get it. That she could not do, for she was afraid to show her face in the hostile crowd. And so the nightmare, as it seemed to her, wore on. Finally, exhausted from the noise and horrible sights in the street below, she fell asleep.

Early the next morning she was awakened by a telephone call from the customers she was to meet. They had arrived during the height of the riot and had gone to bed, disgusted. Soon the firm's chauffeur arrived as arranged, and after a hurried breakfast they left for Cologne, about an hour's drive from Krefeld. The streets were in a shambles. That was the last parcel of goods Lydia ever sold in Germany, for she did not return while Hitler ruled.

While Lydia was dealing with her customers at the warehouse, special agents of the Hitler Party (every firm was forced to employ at least one or two) stood behind the glass partitions, furtively watching the proceedings so they could later report to headquarters.

A well-liked Jewish salesman, a 30-year employee of the firm with which Lydia was doing business, had died the day before. The Nazis posted notices in the offices and warehouses warning the *Aryan* employees that if they attended the funeral, they would be expelled from the party and punished. This infuriated some of the Gentile employees, who had worked with this Jewish colleague for most of their lives and had learned to love and respect him.

Thus, the atmosphere was charged with fear, hatred, suspicion, and danger in Hitler's Germany in 1938.

Her task completed, Lydia quickly left Germany on the first plane back to London, where once again she breathed freely and thanked God for a free country. The memories of that trip to Cologne remained indelibly fixed in her mind, and as she thought of that night in later years, she shuddered at what might have happened to her, in spite of her British passport, which at that time still commanded some respect in Germany.

Soon Mr. Silber was able to produce the same quality goods in British factories and severed all ties with Germany, the country he once loved but which now dealt so treacherously and cruelly with its Jewish citizens.

28

A Giant Stalks the Earth

B Y CHRISTMAS 1938 Jack had decided that his future was in America, where he was anxious to start a new life. It seemed to be God's will for him to go back. Two country churches in South Dakota extended a call to Jack to be their pastor, and the family prepared him for the journey. He was outfitted from head to toe with new clothing, new luggage, and everything else he would need. Jack looked forward to a future full of promise.

But the Lord again said, through the Prophet Isaiah, "my thoughts are not your thoughts, neither are your ways my ways" (Isa. 55:8).

On January 6, 1939 (three months before the Buksbazens' first son, John, was born), Jack sailed for America, full of hopes and dreams, looking forward to a new life in the Lord's work. Like Moses, he was shown the *Promised Land* but was not permitted to enter it.

Jack sadly parted from his mother, to whom he was deeply attached. On leaving the boat, Yente said to her daughter Betty, "Somehow, I don't think I will ever see him again." Further down the river Thames in London, Lydia and Victor, who were late in arriving, reached the boat as it entered a lock, and there they had a ten-minute conversation with Jack from the quay. He was happy and excited and told them he would secure a *call* for Victor from the United States, so that they too could go to the country he had learned to love.

"I am sure," he said to his brother-in-law, "the Lord has a special place of service for you in America." Little did he know of the *call* that awaited him on his arrival in the United States. Lydia too had a strange feeling—that Jack would never see her baby.

January of 1939 went by fast. Due to winter storms, the trans-Atlantic crossing took about 12 days. On the 17th and 18th days after Jack sailed, Yente and the rest of the family were restless at not hearing of his safe arrival. On the 19th day, early in the morning, Yente was so ill at ease that she took the bus from her home in Hutton, Essex, to Walthamstow where Ernest lived.

Ernest, his wife Ella, and his sister Mary, who was visiting them, were having breakfast when the doorbell rang. Ernest went to the door, and a cable from Chicago was delivered to him. Hastily he opened it and read, "Jacob had appendectomy. Passed away. Shall we bury here?" It was signed by Mr. Lewek, President of the Hebrew-Christian Alliance of America.

He was shocked and rooted to the spot, but he acted quickly. Fearing to tell his wife and Mary too abruptly, he stuffed the cable in his pocket and hurried to London. On the way he called Lydia at the office. She had just arrived. When she heard the news, everything went black and she fainted, falling off the chair.

When her co-workers revived her, Lydia spoke to Ernest again, and her mind started working with the whirling speed of one faced with a sudden catastrophe. They recalled that Jack had once mentioned to his mother that the Hebrew-Christian Alliance in Chicago had a plot of ground for the burial of Hebrew Christians in the beautiful Acacia Park Cemetery and that he would like to be buried there, so they composed a reply cable asking that their brother be buried in that cemetery. Then came the sad trek back home to convey the news to the rest of the family that Jack had gone home to be with his Lord.

In the meantime Yente had arrived. She asked Ella if there were any news from Jack and why Ernest was in town so early in the morning. Ella answered truthfully that she did not know, so Yente was about to leave when Lydia and Ernest arrived.

The Faith of Yente

Yente looked at their faces and knew all was not well. Lydia took her gently into the house, sat her down, and started to tell her the contents of the telegram. Before she could say that he had passed away, Yente knew and finished the sentence: "My dear Jack has gone to be with the Lord."

What happened after that will forever be the greatest testimony to Yente's faith. Instead of fainting, as her children expected, she clasped her hands, got down on her knees, raised her head to Heaven, and prayed, "Lord, I thank Thee for Thy wisdom. I will praise Thee at all times. Thou hast given, and Thou hast taken away. Blessed be Thy name."

It seemed that at that moment a host of angels encompassed her round about. They upheld her and gave her supernatural strength. She was calm and composed. "Come, my child," she said to Lydia, "we must think of you and of your child yet to be born. The Lord has taken our Jack away, and now He will give you a son in his place. You must take care of yourself, and I too must take care of you." Together they went to Whitby Moor, their little bungalow home in Hutton, which contained so many memories, both bitter and sweet. They were too grief-stricken and numb to weep. Later when Benjamin, who had received the news on the telephone, arrived home, the floodgates broke and each wept separately, not wanting the others to see. The blow aged Yente overnight. The next morning she awoke after a fitful night, and her hair had taken on a new hue, changing from partly grey to completely white.

The next day yet another drop of bitterness was added to their cup of sorrow. When the mail from the United States arrived, having been delayed by winter storms for several days, there were postcards from Jack with greetings to all the members of the family and a letter telling about the pleasant, though stormy, crossing to America. He said that he was well and happy and looking forward with anticipation to his new life as a preacher and pastor.

Later they learned that when Jack arrived in America, he stopped in New York City to visit some old friends. On the way to his pastorate in South Dakota, he also visited in Chicago. He spent the evening at the home of one of his dear Hebrew-Christian friends, where he was entertained at supper. Later he returned to the Y.M.C.A. for the night, and he was suddenly taken ill with an attack of appendicitis. The details of his sickness never became clear to his family. Apparently, Jack became seriously ill during the night, was unable to notify anyone of his condition, and when the doctor finally arrived, he thought Jack was merely suffering with acute indigestion. When his condition worsened, he was rushed to the hospital, and an emergency appendectomy was performed immediately. However, by this time peritonitis had set in, and then postoperative pneumonia developed.

Feeling that the Lord was going to take him home, Jack called the brethren for prayer and asked to be anointed. He led in the prayer meeting himself, sitting up in the oxygen tent. All the brethren marveled at the testimony of the dying young man. He thanked God for his believing father and mother, who had brought him up in the fear and love of the Lord Jesus Christ. He committed them, his family, and the brethren to his Savior, and then he fell asleep.

Darkening Days

Anyone not living in Europe during those dark days in the latter part of the "terrible 30s" cannot possibly understand the sense of impending doom that hung heavily over the spirits of men. It was as if an evil giant were stalking the earth, gobbling up whole nations along the path. With each meal he seemed to grow stronger, and his appetite became more voracious.

"Who will be the next to become fodder for the giant?" nations small and large asked themselves. The Jews, who were the special object of Hitler's mad obsession, were living in a kind of frenzied nightmare, as when you dream about some wrathful, strong man running after you, but your feet are rooted to the spot and you cannot escape. But this was no dream; this nightmare was gruesomely real.

Like Sheep to the Slaughter

The Hebrew-Christian family of David Fogel, who had lived in Germany for nearly half a century, was now trapped behind those barred doors. One of their sons, Emil, made his way to Palestine. With his bare hands and no money, he worked hard until he was able to send for his wife and children. But his parents and two sisters were trapped in Germany.

The Sitenhofs in England made frantic efforts to rescue their relatives, the Fogels, but red tape enmeshed them more effectively than iron chains could possibly have done. By the time the Fogels finally received permission to come to England, war had broken out. Soon after, the Fogels were imprisoned by the Nazis, and they perished in the cattle car of a train that was taking them to a concentration camp. But they died with a hymn on their lips. A Christian lady who was a friend of the Fogel family witnessed their departure and wrote to the Sitenhofs after the war giving the sad details of their last hours.

She was traveling back to her home on the same train as the Fogels, although she was in a passenger car reserved for Germans, which was ahead of the cattle cars filled with Jews. As she alighted at her station, the strains of a familiar hymn greeted her ears. She walked quickly toward the cattle cars, hoping to get a last glimpse of the Fogel family, but instead she heard their clear voices, above the wailing and moaning of the other doomed Jews, singing,

So take my hands, dear Lord, and lead me on Until my life is ended and then beyond. I cannot walk alone, dear Lord, not one small step, Wherever Thou goest or stayest, I will go with Thee.

Thus David, his wife Dora, and their daughter Hedwig went joyfully home to be with the Lord. Their other daughter, Martha, who was married to a devout German Christian, survived, but not without experiencing the horrors of being persecuted and hunted like a wild animal until the end of the war.

Trapped in Poland

Victor Buksbazen's mother and two sisters were still living in Poland. As the eldest son, he had been the main support of his family since the death of his father in 1920. His sister Hanna was married to a printer, and they had a son Abraham who, before the outbreak of the war, was about four years old. Victor's 19-year-old sister Dora was a student at the Warsaw Polytechnic.

Sensing the approach of the war, Victor and Lydia tried to rescue Dora. Christian friends in England gave her an affidavit and enrolled her as a student at the Reading University in England, but Dora too became entangled in red tape, and before a passport could be granted, the war began. Neither Victor's mother nor his sisters and their families escaped. All perished under Hitler or in Russia while trying to escape.

Munich

The stronger Hitler grew, the more contemptuous he became of men and the decent opinions of the civilized world. He and Goebbels were often heard over the radio frantically proclaiming their threats against the Jews and the "rotten democracies." His henchmen and followers, drunk with power, shouted, "Today Germany belongs to us, tomorrow the whole world." And the world trembled.

For years Hitler had been arming, preferring guns to butter, while the peace-craving nations were weak and unarmed. They wanted peace at all costs. In a last desperate effort, the Prime Minister of England, Neville Chamberlain, and the Prime Minister of France, Edouard Daladier, went to Munich in September 1938 to meet with Hitler and his puppet dictator in Italy, Mussolini. Chamberlain, with his black hat and umbrella, became the symbol of appeasement. They begged for peace. Hitler generously promised to give them peace if they would allow him to gobble up the Sudetenland, a vital section of Czechoslovakia partially populated by people of German origin. That was all he wanted—that, and then peace. Hitler was granted his request.

A few hours later Neville Chamberlain alighted from his plane in London, triumphantly waving a piece of paper signed by the Fuhrer, and announced to a jubilant crowd who came to greet him at the airport, "I have brought peace for our time."

Six months later Hitler marched into what was left of Czechoslovakia and, strutting through the streets of Prague, proclaimed himself protector of that helpless, horror-stricken country. The stunned Czech people stood in the streets of Prague crying unashamedly, their freedom murdered. "Peace for our time" lasted less than six months.

Soon after, Hitler again made it known that his patience was exhausted and unless Poland surrendered Danzig and her Baltic province, he would have to march.

It was then that England awoke. The word *appeasement* become dishonorable.

Realizing that no plea or abject effort of appeasement would stop Hitler, they started arming frantically, seeking at the same time an alliance with Russia against a common foe. But Stalin, to the amazement of the world, suddenly announced that he had concluded a nonaggression pact with Hitler.

On September 1, 1939, the German Wehrmacht swooped down on the borders of Poland, her Panzer divisions and the Luftwaffe raining fire and death on Poland's peaceful villages and towns. After a heroic but brief resistance, Poland succumbed. On September 3 Great Britain declared war with Germany. France followed suit.

Europe was aflame. England, expecting the worst, prepared to live underground in dugouts, known as Anderson shelters. These were provided by the government for the protection of the civil population against air raids. For a time it was comparatively peaceful in England. People began to talk about a "phony war." Yet a devastating and cruel war was being waged in Eastern Europe. After Poland was vanquished, neutral Norway was invaded suddenly and without warning by the Nazi armies. Hitler was now master in Eastern Europe and could turn his attention to the West.

The "phony war" took on a grim and foreboding aspect for the people of Britain. At that time there were thousands of Jewish refugees there who had barely managed to escape annihilation on the European continent. These people were perplexed and apprehensive. Would their terrible enemy reach out his deadly hand and destroy them, even here in England, where they had found friends and protection?

Many of these people, sorely in need of reassurance and comfort, often gathered in the homes of the Sitenhofs and Buksbazens. Those who arrived fearful and depressed left encouraged, their fears dispelled and their spirits directed toward the God of Israel who loved them and gave His all to them and for them.

Perturbed and anxious, their hearts were now open to the Word of God and to the gospel as they had never been before. As they needed the breath of life, likewise they needed faith, and where else could they find it but in the book of life? Those were days when men had to live by faith, if they were to live at all.

29

Yente Finds the City

WITH POLAND PROSTRATE AND DEFEATED and Norway securely in their grip after a treacherous attack, in the spring of 1940 the Nazis turned against the Western allies. Again without warning, they invaded neutral Holland and Belgium. After a brief battle, King Leopold II of Belgium promptly surrendered himself and his army to the Germans. The back door—in fact, the whole rear wall—of France stood wide open to the invader. The Maginot Line was pitifully useless against an enemy coming from the rear. The British expeditionary forces in Europe, together with the remnants of the French, Belgian, and Dutch forces, retreated toward the Channel ports of France and Belgium.

Early in June of 1940, some 330,000 soldiers—almost the entire British army—and some remnants of her allies found themselves trapped on the beaches of Dunkirk with their backs to the sea, encircled by a relentless and confident enemy. One of the most nightmarish and decisive weeks in history ensued.

The men on the beaches of Dunkirk were the pride of British manhood. If they fell into the hands of the enemy, Britain would be at the mercy of the invaders. In a valiant effort to rescue these soldiers, all ferries, transport ships, sporting yachts, and fishing smacks—in fact, anything that could float and take a few men aboard—were rushed to the beaches of Dunkirk.

The world held its breath. Would this be the end of Britain and of freedom in Europe? Freedom hung in the balance. A mighty stream of prayer went up to God from countless hearts everywhere, and those fervent prayers were heard and answered. The English Channel, usually choppy and boisterous at that time of year, was strangely calm. Even the smallest vessels were able to make the trip and rescue soldiers from the beaches. Some of the frail boats managed to cross the Channel several times. Most of the men, about 270,000 in all, were taken off the beaches of Dunkirk and brought home safely. However, their equipment and arms fell into enemy hands.

The Sea Lion in His Lair

While these events were occurring, Yente sat glued to the radio, waiting for every word that came across the waves concerning the turn of events. She neither ate nor drank, but fasted and prayed. She fought for her adopted homeland with the only weapons she had—prayer and faith.

At last a kindly neighbor, seeing Yente's haggard face, brought her tea and biscuits, confidently trusting in the comforting and sustaining virtues of the proverbial British "cup o' tea." "My dear," she coaxed Yente, "drink this, it will do you good." And it always did.

By the middle of June 1940, the *Miracle of Dunkirk* was history—England had her strong sons home again. But with her allies vanquished, Britain stood almost alone and unarmed, facing a deadly enemy who was drunk with victory. Her main defenses were faith, courage, and hope. In the words of her towering leader, Winston Churchill, this was one of the finest hours in England's long history.

The British expected the Nazis to follow up Dunkirk with an invasion of their country. Indeed, the Germans were gathering an invasion fleet in the Channel ports of Europe and mustering their mighty armies for a final blow against Britain, which they dubbed "Operation Sea Lion." The "Sea Lion," roaring defiantly, was preparing to defend himself to the end against all odds. Great roadblocks of solid concrete were set up on highways, fields, and meadows.

The Battle of Britain

Lydia and Victor had given up their apartment and planned to move in with Ernest. Soon after the war broke out, American authorities, anticipating heavy air raids in Britain, persuaded all United States citizens to return home while transportation was still available. Ernest's wife Ella, for the sake of their six-month-old son David, returned home to live with her parents in California.

In May 1940, Mary too had a son, Harold, but all did not go well for her and her family. Her husband, who suffered with heart trouble, suddenly collapsed and died when the baby was two months old. Mary was so grief-stricken that she and the baby had to be hospitalized in a private nursing home. The funeral was on August 10, and Yente was too shocked to attend. That day she had a dizzy spell in her garden and fell into a six-foot ditch.

The following Monday, August 12, was Lydia's birthday. Not having heard anything definite from her mother about her condition, other than that she did not feel well, she went to Hutton, where she discovered that Yente had had a stroke and was in bed and alone. She called Benjamin, who came at once, and since Yente obviously required skilled nursing, they decided to have her transported by ambulance to the nursing home in London where Mary and her baby were being cared for. Thus Lydia could look after them both.

It was on that day that the battle of Britain began in earnest. Great swarms of German bombers came roaring across the Channel and darkened the skies. Their sinister drone filled every heart with grim foreboding. Soon the shrill sounds of warning sirens were heard across London.

The ride with Yente in the ambulance to the nursing home was a nightmare. As they started, the shrill, ear-piercing air raid warning sounded; then the roar of the enemy planes was heard. But the ambulance continued on until it reached the nursing home.

Day after day the enemy planes came in full force, sometimes more than a thousand at a time. But the British airmen, reinforced by Allied pilots who escaped to England, were able to destroy hundreds of planes time and again. It was not unusual to see aerial dogfights taking place in the skies over London and its suburbs, with pilots bailing out of the planes to be killed or captured on the ground below.

Winston Churchill, the man whom God raised up during that hour of grave peril to steel the will of his people for the defense of their country, said concerning the men of the Royal Air Force, "Seldom in the field of human conflict have so many owed so much to so few." Those knights of the air helped to turn the tide of events and said to the tyrant, "It shall not be."

Later, when the Luftwaffe realized they could not bomb London into submission during daylight hours, they started their raids after sunset and continued their work of destruction through the night. The hordes of enemy planes came as regularly as clockwork, dropping their loads of heavy bombs or incendiary missiles, shattering and burning whole sections of London and killing and maiming thousands.

As soon as the sirens sounded at dusk, or even before, people rushed to take shelter in places specially prepared for the public. Others went to the Anderson shelters in their own back yards. There, together with their young children and babies, they huddled together in the dark and dank quarters, trying to make themselves as comfortable as possible with blankets and hot water bottles. The shelters had been built for the First World War, when an air raid lasted no longer than two or three hours.

In 1940, however, the air raids began at 4 p.m. and continued until 8 a.m. the next day, meaning that somehow, as cramped as these shelters were, sleeping accommodations had to be made, at least for the children. Bunks, often no wider than 15 inches, were made in which people could stretch their weary bodies for at least part of the 14 hours they might be in the damp shelters.

Some played games or talked, and others sang hymns or prayed. London became a city of cave dwellers. These were nerve-racking nights filled with the constant blast of falling bombs, the answering fire of antiaircraft guns, and the crackle of burning timbers. The skies were illumined and crisscrossed by innumerable searchlights. London was ablaze.

In the morning, when at last the all-clear signal sounded, the citizenry emerged, the night dampness and chill still in their bones, grimy, red-eyed, and tired. Their first concern was always to see if their homes were still standing. Many were filled with joy when they discovered their houses still intact; but others, coming out of their shelters, found their homes burned or blasted. Sometimes the electricity, gas, or water mains were damaged, and no hot meals could be prepared. When the water reservoirs were hit, the misery became even more acute.

But London, determined to survive, carried on with a grim kind of humor, courageous and defiant. Men and nations are tested in days of trial and supreme peril. It is then that the true nature and inherent strength of those tested become evident. Britain stood her test and passed it nobly.

London and outlying sections on the Thames estuary were bombed daily. Thousands of homes, public buildings, churches, and hospitals went up in flames. Every night men, women, and children were killed by enemy bombs or injured by fragments of antiaircraft shells. Ghostlike streets were gutted and lifeless. Survivors were removed to less dangerous parts of the country.

Ernest, who was an air raid warden and a chaplain apart from his church pastorate, daily conducted the funerals of bombing victims. Sometimes whole families were wiped out.

At first the noise and blasts were terrifying. Children screamed in terror. Some of the first words Lydia's son John learned to say were *blackout* and *bomb*.

Meanwhile, in the nursing home Yente was very sick. The bombing worried her, so her ears were plugged; but she could still hear the noise. Patients who were able to walk unassisted to the basement shelter were encouraged to do so. But by that time Yente could not stand on her feet, and her speech was impaired.

Eventually Mary and her poorly nourished infant left the nursing home and joined Lydia's household, but she was too grief-stricken to look after her son. Every morning, with John in the pram, Lydia took chicken broth to the nursing home for her mother, but her condition grew worse. Yente begged to be taken to Ernest's home, since she did not want to remain on the third floor of the nursing home during those dreadful raids that lasted for eight hours or more and then through the night. Confusion and chaos reigned everywhere.

Victor's activities on behalf of The British Jews Society were, of necessity, curtailed. As a "friendly alien" (Polish), he could travel freely in so-called "nondefense areas," but the entire coastline was declared a "defense area." This meant that he could not go to many of the churches where he had been invited to speak before the air raids began. Nor was it possible to visit the heavily bombed and burned out East End of London, where so many Jewish people lived.

At that time the Lord laid it on the heart of a missionary society in America to extend a call to Victor, which he gladly accepted, although the Buksbazens had no idea when they could obtain visas and secure transportation to America across the submarine-infested Atlantic. But in this, too, Victor and Lydia experienced the truth that with God all things are possible.

Events followed each other swiftly in the late autumn of 1940. Daylight was so short that it seemed almost a miracle how the Lord enabled Lydia to do all the things that were needed: feed, wash, and comfort two babies, look after a household, two men, and her sick mother in the nursing home, and comfort her sister in her bereavement. All this time London was experiencing the worst air raids yet. Those were days that tried the hearts of even the strongest. Blessed was the person whose heart was stayed upon Jehovah (Isa. 26:3). "God is our refuge and strength, a very present help in trouble. Therefore will not we fear" (Ps. 46:1-2).

Yente Finds the City

Yente was not improving. How could she? She needed peace and quiet to recover from a stroke such as she had suffered, but instead there were the explosions of bombs and the wailing of air raid sirens. To make things worse, medical aid was hard to obtain, since nurses and doctors alike were evacuated from London at the beginning of the bombing or were in military service.

Yente was dying and she knew it, so she begged to go back to her beloved Whitby Moor in Hutton. Unfortunately it was a "defense area" where large antiaircraft guns paraded up and down and shot at the planes as they came from the continent to prevent them from reaching the heart of London. The blasts from the antiaircraft firing were often more terrifying than the bombs themselves.

Lydia went back to Hutton with her mother and the baby in an ambulance with a large red cross on the roof, and she tried to nurse her as best she could, although she had no nursing experience at all. Victor and Ernest stayed in Walthamstow, where Ernest had his church, only half of which was still standing. Large sheets of tarpaulin covered the gaping holes where walls had once been, and the services were sometimes conducted under a blue sky, since the roof had been badly damaged. Those were grim days indeed.

By the end of August the strain was too much for Lydia. Betty and her husband, who were keeping house in the country for a farmer, relieved her for a few weeks, and then she resumed the heartbreaking task of nursing the mother she loved so dearly. Yente's swallowing muscles became paralyzed, and she grew weaker with each passing day. She had to be restrained in bed during the terrible night raids, since the blasts could have thrown her out of bed. The agony of seeing her suffer was great for the family, and coupled with the strain of the air raid conditions, Lydia sometimes prayed, "Oh Lord, do not let this continue—give her peace and rest."

At last an elderly nurse was found, and a small thatched cottage was rented deep in the country where the doctor said she might be able to recover, since it was away from the bombing and the big guns. Benjamin also went along.

Again the ambulance arrived, and they carried her gently on the stretcher. Then the wailing of the sirens started. "Never mind," she said as she kissed her child, "there is rest and peace with the Lord, and I am going to Him." She was losing ground steadily. Her paralyzed throat muscles did not permit her to receive nourishment. A few days later Yente lapsed into a coma. Seven weeks of starvation were more than her frail body could endure.

Then the Lord swung open the gates of Heaven to His journey-worn handmaiden. The pilgrim was home! At last Yente entered the city of her longings and prayers, the "city which hath foundations, whose builder and maker is God" (Heb. 11:10).

MORE BOOKS FROM
THE FRIENDS OF ISRAEL

by Bruce Scott

THE FEASTS OF ISRAEL
Seasons of the Messiah
Many of the Bible's most incredible prophecies about Christ are intricately hidden within the Jewish holidays and feasts of the Old Testament. That's where you'll find little-known yet astounding pictures of Christ's deity, His death and resurrection, and even His Second Coming and future reign as King of kings and Lord of lords. You'll discover that much of what Jesus said and did—which seems mysterious to us today—suddenly makes complete sense. Don't miss any part of the greatest story ever told.

ISBN-10: 0-915540-14-2, # B65
ISBN-13: 978-0-915540-14-3

by Zvi Kalisher

THE BEST OF ZVI
This unique sampler of Zvi's experiences sharing his faith will inspire and encourage you as you see God's infinite love, wisdom, and power in action. Walk through the streets of Jerusalem with Zvi as he converses with people of all backgrounds in all types of places—army camps, hospitals, religious schools, synagogues, workplaces, and even people's homes.

ISBN-10: 0-915540-59-2, # B71
ISBN-13: 978-0-915540-59-4

by Elwood McQuaid

THE ZION CONNECTION

Elwood McQuaid takes a thoughtful, sensitive look at relations between Jewish people and evangelical Christians, including the controversial issues of anti-Semitism, the rise of Islam, the right of Jewry to a homeland in the Middle East, and whether Christians should try to reach Jewish people with the gospel message—and how.

ISBN-10: 0-915540-40-1, # B61
ISBN-13: 978-0-915540-40-2

II PETER: STANDING FAST IN THE LAST DAYS

- How can we live for God during these climactic days before the Lord returns?
- How can we identify false teachers and charlatans?
- How can we understand what eternity holds?

This excellent volume provides answers to these important questions from the little but powerful Bible book of 2 Peter. Its timely message will become an invaluable addition to your life as well as your personal library.

ISBN-10: 0-915540-65-7, # B79
ISBN-13: 978-0-915540-65-5

by David M. Levy

THE TABERNACLE:

SHADOWS OF THE MESSIAH

This superb work on Israel's wilderness Tabernacle explores in depth the service of the priesthood and the significance of the sacrifices. The well-organized content and numerous illustrations will open new vistas of biblical truth as ceremonies, sacrifices, and priestly service reveal the perfections of the Messiah

ISBN-10: 0-915540-17-7, # B51
ISBN-13: 978-0-915540--17-4

by Renald E. Showers

THE MOST HIGH GOD

A Commentary on the Book of Daniel
This clear, concise, and consistently premillennial exposition is one of the finest commentaries on the book of Daniel available today. It sheds tremendous light on prophecy, the Times of the Gentiles, and other key portions of the prophetic Word.
ISBN-10: 0-915540-30-4, # B26
ISBN-13: 978-0-915540-30-3

THE FOUNDATIONS OF FAITH VOL. ONE

With execptional fidelity to Scripture, Dr. Showers tackles Bibliology and Christology—the doctrines of the Bible and Messiah. Learn what the Bible says about itself, why no other book in the world is like it, the differences between specific and general revelation, what the Bible teaches about Christ, and much more.
ISBN-10: 0-915540-77-0, # B89 (hardcover)
ISBN-13: 978-0-915540-77-8

by Victor Buksbazen

ISAIAH'S MESSIAH

From the scholarly pen of Dr. Victor Buksbazen comes an outstanding work on a premier section of the prophetic Hebrew Scriptures, Isaiah 52—53. This superb and attractive little volume masterfully answers the all-important Jewish question, Of whom did the prophet speak? Of Israel, as many rabbis teach, or of Messiah? In an eloquent yet in-depth, verse-by-verse exposition, Dr. Buksbazen shows how Isaiah 53—the only section of the Bible never read in the synagogue—speaks unequivocally of Jesus.
ISBN-10: 0-915540-75-4, # B87 (hardcover)
ISBN-13: 978-0-915540-75-4

by Steve Herzig

JEWISH CULTURE & CUSTOMS
A Sampler of Jewish Life
Every area of Jewish life radiates with symbolism.
Hundreds of fascinating traditions date back thousands of years. How did these customs get started?
What special meaning do they hold? And what can
they teach us? Explore the answers to these questions in this enjoyable sampler of the colorful
world of Judaism. You'll see the Bible and
Christianity in a whole new light.
ISBN-10: 0-915540-31-2, # B68
ISBN-13: 978-0-915540-31-0

For current prices, order by credit card, or to obtain
a complete catalog of all the resources available from
The Friends of Israel, call us at **800-345-8461**; visit our
Web store at **www.foi.org**; or write us at **P.O. Box
908, Bellmawr, NJ 08099.**